A Message to the **Youth of India**

Bhakti Vikāsa Swami

Plus

Śrīla Prabhupāda On India

Quotations from the founder-*ācārya* of the International Society for Krishna Consciousness

With commentary by Bhakti Vikāsa Swami

A Message to the Youth of India (English)
ISBN 978-81-908292-3-6

Previous printings: 45,000 copies
Second printing of revised edition (2017): 20,000 copies

www.bvks.com
books@bvks.com

Also available in Bengali, Gujarati, Hindi, Marathi, Tamil, and Telugu

Published by Bhakti Vikas Trust, Surat, India

Printed in India

Contents

About Śrīla Prabhupāda

His Divine Grace A.C. Bhaktivedanta Swami Prabhupāda appeared in this world in 1896 in Calcutta (now Kolkata).

In 1922, after completing college, he first met his guru, Śrīla Bhaktisiddhānta Sarasvatī Ṭhākura—a prominent religious scholar and the founder of the Gauḍīya Maṭha spiritual institution—who entreated him to dedicate his life to broadcasting Vedic knowledge in the English language. Śrīla Prabhupāda became his follower and, in 1933, was formally initiated as his disciple.

In the following years, Śrīla Prabhupāda wrote a commentary on the *Bhagavad-gītā,* rendered assistance to the Gauḍīya Maṭha, and in 1944 started *Back to Godhead,* an English fortnightly magazine. Single-handedly, he edited it, typed the manuscripts, checked the galley proofs, and even distributed the individual copies. Today, *Back to Godhead* is being continued by his followers.

In 1950, Śrīla Prabhupāda retired from married life to devote more time to study, writing, and preaching. For that purpose, he travelled to the holy city of Vṛndāvana, where he lived in humble circumstances in the historic temple of Rādhā-Dāmodara.

In 1959, Śrīla Prabhupāda accepted *sannyāsa* (formal renunciation of family life for full dedication to spiritual pursuits). At Rādhā-Dāmodara, he began work on a multivolume commentated translation of the eighteen-thousand-verse *Śrīmad-Bhāgavatam*. He also wrote *Easy Journey to Other Planets*.

In August 1965, after publishing three volumes of the *Bhāgavatam*, Śrīla Prabhupāda set out to the United States to fulfil the mission of his guru. When he first arrived, by freighter, he was practically penniless. After almost a year of great difficulty, in July of 1966 he established the International Society for Krishna Consciousness.

Before his passing away, on 14 November 1977, Śrīla Prabhupāda had guided the Society and seen it grow to a worldwide confederation of more than one hundred ashrams, schools, temples, institutes, and farm communities. He had also inspired the construction of several major temples in India, including the international headquarters of ISKCON, at Māyāpur, West Bengal, the site of a developing Vedic city. In Vṛndāvana, Uttar Pradesh, is the magnificent Kṛṣṇa-Balarāma Temple. ISKCON also has established several other major temples throughout the world.

Yet Śrīla Prabhupāda's most significant contribution was his books. He wrote more than fifty volumes of authoritative commentated translations and summary studies of the philosophical and religious classics of India. Highly respected by scholars for their authority, depth, and clarity, over five hundred million copies have been printed in more than eighty languages. The Bhaktivedanta Book Trust, established in 1972 to publish the works of His Divine Grace A.C. Bhaktivedanta Swami Prabhupāda, has thus become the world's largest publisher of books in the field of Indian religion and philosophy.

Despite his advanced age, Śrīla Prabhupāda circled the globe fourteen times in just twelve years, on lecture tours that brought him to six continents. And amidst such a rigorous schedule, he continued to write prolifically. Indeed, Śrīla Prabhupāda's writings constitute a veritable library of Vedic philosophy, religion, literature, and culture.

Books by Śrīla Prabhupāda

Bhagavad-gītā As It Is
Śrīmad-Bhāgavatam (18 vols.; with disciples)
Śrī Caitanya-caritāmṛta (9 vols.)
Kṛṣṇa, The Supreme Personality of Godhead
Teachings of Lord Caitanya
The Nectar of Devotion
The Nectar of Instruction
Śrī Īśopaniṣad
Light of the Bhāgavata
Easy Journey to Other Planets
The Science of Self Realization
Kṛṣṇa Consciousness: The Topmost Yoga System
Perfect Questions, Perfect Answers
Teachings of Lord Kapila, the Son of Devahūti
Transcendental Teachings of Prahlāda Mahārāja
Teachings of Queen Kuntī
Kṛṣṇa, the Reservoir of Pleasure
The Path of Perfection
Life Comes from Life
Message of Godhead
The Perfection of Yoga
Beyond Birth and Death

On the Way to Kṛṣṇa
Rāja-Vidyā: The King of Knowledge
Elevation to Kṛṣṇa Consciousness
Kṛṣṇa Consciousness: The Matchless Gift
Nārada-bhakti-sūtra (with disciples)
Mukunda-mālā-stotra (with disciples)
A Second Chance
The Journey of Self-Discovery
The Laws of Nature: An Infallible Justice
Renunciation Through Wisdom
Civilization and Transcendence
The Quest for Enlightenment
Dharma: The Way of Transcendence
Introduction to Bhagavad-gītā
The Hare Kṛṣṇa Challenge
Gītāra Gāna (Bengali)
Vairāgya-vidyā (Bengali)
Buddhi-yoga (Bengali)
Bhakti-ratna-bolī (Bengali)
Back to Godhead magazine (founder)

To order, visit www.indiabbt.com.
Or contact your nearest ISKCON centre.

About Bhakti Vikāsa Swami

The author was born in Britain in 1957 and joined ISKCON in London in 1975. Later that year he was formally accepted as a disciple of His Divine Grace A. C. Bhaktivedanta Swami Prabhupāda, the founder-*ācārya* of ISKCON, and named Ilāpati dāsa.

From 1977 to 1979 Ilāpati dāsa was based in India, mostly travelling in West Bengal distributing Śrīla Prabhupāda's books. He spent the following ten years helping to pioneer ISKCON's preaching in Bangladesh, Malaysia, Myanmar, and Thailand.

In 1989 he was granted the order of *sannyāsa*, receiving the name Bhakti Vikāsa Swami, and again made his base in India. Since then he has preached Kṛṣṇa consciousness throughout the subcontinent, lecturing in English, Hindi, and Bengali. He also spends a few months each year preaching in the West. His television lectures in Hindi have reached millions worldwide.

Bhakti Vikāsa Swami has written fourteen books, which have been translated into over twenty languages, with more than seven hundred thousand in print.

Books Authored by Bhakti Vikāsa Swami

A Beginner's Guide to Kṛṣṇa Consciousness
A Message to the Youth of India
Brahmacarya in Kṛṣṇa Consciousness
Glimpses of Traditional Indian Life
Jaya Śrīla Prabhupāda!
Lekha-mālā
Mothers and Masters
My Memories of Śrīla Prabhupāda
On Pilgrimage in Holy India
On Speaking Strongly in Śrīla Prabhupāda's Service
Patropadeśa
Śrī Bhaktisiddhānta Vaibhava (3 volumes)
Śrī Caitanya Mahāprabhu
Vaṁśīdāsa Bābājī
Vaiṣṇava Śikhā o Sādhana (Bengali)

Books Edited or Compiled by Bhakti Vikāsa Swami

Rāmāyaṇa
The Story of Rasikānanda
Gauḍīya Vaiṣṇava Padyāvalī (Bengali)

Please visit www.bvks.com or mail to bvksbooks@gmail.com to order the above books.

Preface

It may pertinently be asked, "How is it that a foreigner has the audacity to comment about India and Indians? This Bhakti Vikāsa Swami even strongly criticizes and presumes to instruct us!"

In reply, I submit that I have been following traditional Indian culture for most of my life. I have travelled throughout most of India, mixed with all kinds of people at all levels of society, and learned two Indian languages. Having visited many other countries also, and observed the people of different lands, I am convinced that the original Indian culture is the best the world has ever known. Furthermore, in today's troubled world India's spiritual message is vitally needed. It is thus regrettable that in this hour of need, when Indians should be distributing their ancient wisdom, they are instead giving it up.

If my words seem harsh, it is not out of antagonism, but from a hope that India will revive her lost glory and stand as a leader among nations. As a sannyasi, it is my duty to instruct. Moreover, the topics in this book are either based on or are direct quotations from the teachings of His Divine Grace A.C. Bhaktivedanta Swami Prabhupāda, the founder-*ācārya* of ISKCON. Admittedly, I am a very insignificant soul, but my spiritual master, Śrīla Prabhupāda, is a great world *ācārya*. Whatever he says should be taken seriously.

I thus request the readers not to be disturbed by the strong statements contained herein, but to try to perceive the truth in them. I am confident that, if received properly, this book can do much good for India. I pray to Lord Śrī Kṛṣṇa, the Supreme Personality of Godhead, that He bless me, as well as the readers of this book, the land of India, and all people in the universe. If He so desires, this book can help contribute to the ongoing reawakening of the world's oldest and greatest civilization.

oṁ tat sat

Bhakti Vikāsa Swami
Vadodara, 6 October 1993

Introduction

This work is in two parts. The first, *A Message to the Youth of India*, an essay by Bhakti Vikāsa Swami, brings together most of the points that His Divine Grace A. C. Bhaktivedanta Swami Prabhupāda taught about India. The second is a selection of quotations about India from Śrīla Prabhupāda's extensive writings, conversations, and lectures.*

In the early 1970s, having established Kṛṣṇa consciousness in the West, Śrīla Prabhupāda started concentrating his attention on India. He told his disciples, "My spiritual master wanted me to preach in the Western countries. Now that I have done that, I want to preach in India." Yet in the 70s many Indians, suspecting that the Westerners' *bhakti* was merely a passing fashion, did not take ISKCON very seriously.

Now, a generation later, the foreign devotees have remained, and acceptance of ISKCON has grown. Many Indians are now initiated disciples of Western-born devotees. Educated Indians, many of whom were apathetic to *sanātana-dharma,* are again taking pride in their own culture. Like it or not, religion has come to the forefront of national life.

---

* Some of these quotations, especially from conversations, have been largely reworked for clarity of presentation. References to their original sources are given at the back of the book.

One reason for this is the inspiration generated by outsiders' continued interest in Indian spirituality. The foreign members of ISKCON have particularly impressed Indians with their implicit faith in *śāstra* (especially *Bhagavad-gītā* and *Śrīmad-Bhāgavatam*), their having renounced meat-eating, gambling, the taking of intoxicants, and illicit sex, their austerity and dedication—for instance, members of ISKCON rise daily by 4:00 a.m.—and their adoption of Vedic practices (Indian-style dress, food, and so on). Such committed adherence to genuine Vedic traditions establishes ISKCON's authenticity in contrast to cheap, imitation versions of dharma marketed by pseudo swamis.

Śrīla Prabhupāda often expressed Lord Caitanya's desire that Indians seriously practice Kṛṣṇa consciousness. He had great hope that ISKCON would help India to reverse her lamentable fall into materialism and realize her identity as the spiritual leader of the world.

Not only young people but all classes of Indians will benefit from reading this book. Yet, because the students of today are the leaders of tomorrow, it especially behooves the educated youth of India to deeply ponder this message and apply it practically in their life.

A Message to the Youth of India

A Message to the Youth of India

India—ancient, modern, mystical, alive. A vast land of lofty mountains, broad plains, mighty rivers, throbbing cities. A people searching for identity in a changing world. A land of contradictions, which if overcome could result in India's bursting forth as a leader among nations.

This India, incomparable and unique, is more diverse than any other nation on earth. Over a billion people, of multiple languages, castes, opinions, and creeds, are squeezed together, struggling to survive. Although the country always seems on the verge of exploding into sectarian violence, an intrinsic oneness, a sense of being Indian, subtly binds her people together. That "Indian-ness" is a legacy of her timeless culture—the world's oldest, most elaborate, and most sophisticated. That culture was distinguished by its deep-rooted spirituality and sense of dharma, characterized by inherent faith in God and the Vedas, and in observance of Vedic injunctions as a sacred duty.

But modern India is definitely a land of change. Change is the way of the world, and nothing new to India. Recently this change has been decorated by the word *progress*. Unfortunately, in terms of actual human civilization and happiness, the process of change in India has been one of gradual degradation.

Since the beginning of Kali-yuga, five thousand years ago, ungodly forces have been eroding India's religious sanctity from within. Kali-yuga's influence began with the downfall of the once saintly *brāhmaṇa* community. The original *varṇāśrama* system allowed all classes to be trained according to individual qualities and abilities, and thus even persons from lower families, if possessing an intellectual and virtuous disposition, could be trained as *brāhmaṇas*. But later, the distinguishing of caste merely on the basis of birth led to exploitation, instead of the cooperation for which *varṇāśrama* was intended. Consequently, Hindu society became pervaded by empty ritualism within the upper castes, discontent among the lower castes, and lack of genuine spirituality throughout.

A thousand years ago, Bhārata, which had once ruled the world but was now internally sick and weak, fell to invaders. The aggressors, having gained political control by rule of arms, solidified their position by promoting their own faith, especially among the oppressed, lower-caste Hindus, many of whom readily abandoned the religion of their forefathers to instead eat cows and hate Vedic deities.

Later on, the British intelligently ascertained that the Hindus' tremendous cultural strength derived from their implicit faith in brahminical sanctity and

Vedic injunctions. Hence, the foreign rulers further accelerated India's decline by deliberately attacking and undermining Indian thought and civilization. "Everything Indian is inferior. Everything Western is best," they taught.

Although the British are now gone from India, their legacy yet remains. They de-Indianized India so well that their disciples—educated Indians—have become the new gurus of Westernization. Hence, Indians have largely lost their glorious heritage of thousands of years. Hardly anyone is serious about preserving the unique legacy of transcendental knowledge and enlightened tradition that characterized Indian civilization. It is highly regrettable that Indians are largely ignorant of and uninterested in the incomparable civilization of their forefathers. While maintaining some sentiment for their spiritual and cultural roots, they are firmly committed to pursuing the materialistic paradigm dictated by the West, and thus they accept—practically as a new dharma—Western ways of dress, thought, and behavior. Consequently, a few decades of independence have degraded India more than a thousand years of foreign rule. Although politically free, India has become a slave of foreign ideas.*

---

* For a summary of the British attitude, see: Satsvarūpa dāsa Goswami "The First Indologists," in the appendix of *Readings in Vedic Literature* (Los Angeles: Bhaktivedanta Book Trust, 1990).

After attaining independence, India sought Western-style affluence through industrialization. A new educational machinery was designed to produce innumerable workers blindly dedicated to a massive, complex social system based on profit and exploitation. Ancient values were undermined and the natural environment was raped. Almost all aspects of Indian life have changed radically, from eating and dressing, to social conduct and values. The India of just a generation ago was another world, a different scene. Day by day, yesteryear's culture is being hammered into oblivion. In the land of religion, the land of wisdom, young people are ignorant of the rishis and *ācāryas* and instead idolize monkeylike music and cinema stars. The exalted lifestyle of the past is largely forgotten, as modern Indians prefer to be meat-eaters and drunkards.

Despite all this, Indians are still Indians (although perhaps not quite sure what it means to be Indian). Their attempt to become sahibs is simply artificial—and a poor imitation—for even though trying hard, they cannot become fully Westernized. Caught between tradition and modernity, India is left with the worst of both worlds.

Although most modern Hindus retain a little interest in their dharma, generally they are overwhelmingly concerned with earning money and pursuing artificial standards of living. And while India's recent economic progress has been remarkable, still, amid dreams of a future high-tech paradise, the reality for most remains a daily struggle for survival. Far from enjoying the luxury portrayed in cinemas and on TV, the majority of Indians still struggle to procure basic food, clothing, and shelter. Crores continue to live in poverty, with perhaps a few electronic gadgets meant to keep them happy.

Nevertheless, hope prevails, and "Change! Change! Change!" is the order of the day. Everything alters so rapidly that we are left mentally breathless, unable to imagine what will come next. There is no time to consider whether the changes are for better or for worse—although in terms of actual human happiness and higher values they are clearly mostly for worse. Perhaps more than anywhere else, in India the constant materialistic propaganda from the mass media has made people lusty, greedy, and nasty, with an overwhelming trend toward petty selfishness.

The break from conservatism is most clearly expressed in the quest for sex, which has become ridiculously overstressed, particularly via movies and modern Western-style music. Today's youth have unprecedented scope for indulging in sex, but that has not made them happy. Pristine Indian culture teaches the virtues of moderation and self-control, and the perils of excessively emphasizing sex. Sex may seem like harmless pleasure, but if indulged in illicitly (i.e., outside of marriage, or in perverted ways) it creates innumerable problems both for the involved individuals and the broader society—as the entire world, and particularly India, is experiencing today.*

Promotion of lust and selfishness degrades humans to the level of beasts, as is widely observed in the character of Indian students today. Whereas traditional Indian education imparted character training and knowledge of God, modern schools not only fail to uphold moral principles, but even promote the rot. So-called education is conducted as a business and teaches that man evolved by chance from monkeys. "No need of God"—no mention of God. "Science is God." "Science will solve all problems" (a hopeless hope). Not only from the TV and cinema but even at school, many youth learn to lie, cheat, brag, speak foully, quarrel, fight, make politics, smoke, drink, take drugs, and indulge in sex. Far from helping their inmates, educational institutions mould them for a life of suffering to fulfil the demands of a society that enslaves its members to lifelong inhumanly hard work. Students are under tremendous pressure to be successful in their studies. Although cutting a "cool" profile on campus, they are internally racked by insecurity, tension, depression, confusion, and frustration—as evidenced by frightening rates of suicide, drug and alcohol abuse, and psychiatric disturbance among youth.

---

* For the positive, spiritual alternative to entanglement in lust and sex, see *Brahmacarya in Kṛṣṇa Consciousness* by Bhakti Vikāsa Swami.

At home also, numerous young people are unhappy. They cannot understand, nor be understood by, their elders. They enjoy motorbikes, mobile phones, computers, and iPods the way their parents toyed with transistor radios. The world is open for today's liberated youth—alcohol, drugs, pornography, loose sex, violence. Some parents try to protect their offspring by imposing restrictions. But the youth consider such parents to be suppressive guardians of an old-fashioned morality that they don't want imposed on them: "Why should I do what you say? I'm young, strong, healthy, and want to enjoy. Why shouldn't I? I can look after myself. I don't need you!" Who can stop them? "Jump on a motorbike and hit the road! We'll dress as we like, think as we like, do as we like." The older generation laments, "Our children don't care for what we say. They don't relate to us." But if parents are unable to give any clear direction to their wards, what should they expect?

If the older generation is highly materialistic, absorbed in maintaining and improving a comfortable standard of living, how can they expect their progeny to have finer values? In the unrelenting quest for "Money! Money! Money!" where is the question of right and wrong? "Right" has come to mean succeeding materially; "wrong" means to fail. Moral instructions are imparted as a convenience in an attempt to keep offspring in line. Naturally, to give pious speeches yet set an example of selfishness cannot dupe the educated youth of today. If they are sceptical, disenchanted, misguided—or out-and-out materialists, greedy, or even violent—it is at least partly because the previous generation contributed toward spoiling their character.

Factually, many parents hardly care if their children become degraded, even preferring them to be modern, sinful, mean, and sharp enough for the rat race. Such parents don't mind what kind of job their offspring perform as long as it brings money. They are eager to send their sons, and even daughters, overseas for the sake of dollars and prestige and are not bothered if their children thereby become totally Westernized and degraded. And increasing numbers of ungrateful offspring reap huge salaries yet keep it for themselves, neglecting and even insulting the very parents who sacrificed so much for them.

But while most young people dream of excelling in studies and going overseas, or at least getting a good job at home, for many the reality is bitter. Every year thousands of bright young men and women, having worked so hard and so long for their prized certificate of graduation, then search strenuously in hope of finding a job—yet even if they get one, they often earn less than persons who are hardly literate.

And yet another anxiety for young people is uncertainty about their future marriage. Everyone hopes for an agreeable spouse but simultaneously fears the worst—an unfaithful or incompatible partner. Especially, young women hope and fear more. Every girl dreams of a husband who will love and care for her, but such romantic dreams too often become nightmares. The husband may be a drunkard, may harass his wife's family for dowry, may cruelly beat her, or worse. At the wedding everyone is exuberant and optimistic, but there is no certainty about what the future will bring, for modern-day family life is all too often not "home sweet home."

Family used to mean uncles, aunts, cousins, widows, and in-laws living together. But the demands of city life, combined with the selfishness of consumer society, have caused the demise of the joint family. Now family is *ham do hamāre do:* "We are two and ours are two." Whereas the joint family functioned on cooperation between many members, with juniors trained to respect elders and to maintain them in old age, the new spirit is: "Care for as few as possible. Throw out your parents and have only one or two children." Family values have drastically declined, as evidenced by the increasing rate of divorce. For thousands of years, divorce simply did not exist amongst Hindus, but nowadays it is rapidly becoming like the West: a little squabble and spouses are ready to finish the whole thing.

The moral position of Indian women has significantly degraded. In orthodox Indian culture, virtuous women were revered as sacred—protected and adored for their chastity and motherly sacrifice. Men were trained to see all women except their wife as mothers. But respect for women is now "outdated." Girls are no longer taught *lajjā nārī bhūṣaṇam*, "Shyness is the ornament of women," but are encouraged to wear sexually provocative clothing. Women mix freely with men, and unmarried couples flirt in public. Men view such cheap women simply as objects of sex enjoyment, and hence, young women must now live in fear of molestation.

Like it or not, today's youth are radically different from countless former generations. With the latest fashion clothes and hairstyle, they zoom around on tinny motorbikes, making a big show as if they were Bollywood stars. Some are totally corrupt and spoiled. In some cases, the impressionable minds of students are perverted by gangster-type politicians, who deliberately turn their victims into anti-social monsters. Such lawless young devils have no respect for their professors, fellow students, or anyone else. Always ready to inflict violence on anybody who even verbally opposes them, they forcibly impose strikes at whim, regularly terrorize and disrupt campus life, spoil the morale and good name of educational institutions, and generally take pleasure in making others' lives miserable.

Of course, only a small percentage of young people are outright rogues and ruffians. Indeed, it is a great credit to the youth of India that despite so many bad influences they are not more spoiled. The vast majority are actually fairly decent folk. For even now, the tendency of Indians is to be religious. Their cultural background gives them an inherent, if often dormant, faith in God. After all, India is *puṇya-bhūmi, dharma-bhūmi.* But exposure to innumerable nonsensical ideas has Indians, especially the youth, asking, "Is there really a God? Can the existence of God be proved? Why should we believe all these things? Are we supposed to be just like Westerners? Even if we want to be completely Westernized, is it possible for us? Even if it is possible, is it desirable? What about our ancient customs and heritage? Can't we take the good things of Indian life and mix them with the best of the West?" Fearing ridicule, pious young persons may even conceal their religious tendencies. The spiritual aspirations of India's youth are subverted by the social pressure of materialism, while at every moment their base desires are being fueled. Therefore we find that today's youth of India are at best simply confused, and at worst, demons in human form. Overall, most youngsters are still good at heart but greatly misguided by materialistic propaganda.

Having read this far, the reader might justly challenge, "So exactly what *is* your message to the youth of India?" Our recommendation is: Don't be fooled by *māyā* (illusion). Since young people are easily enamoured by the glitter of material life, they think, "If I get a good job, work hard, and earn good money, I'll be a success. I'll be happy." But that is a foolish hope. Since time immemorial, everyone has been trying to be happy in this ephemeral world yet no one has ever succeeded. As eternal souls (*ātmā*), we belong to the spiritual realm and can be happy only by performing spiritual activities. Hence, to be attracted to the glimmer of materialism is not very intelligent.

So please don't get caught on the superficial platform. Understand that your body is not the real you. You were not made to enjoy matter. You are a pure *ātmā* and have no intrinsic connection with this material world. In the deepest sense, you are not even Indian. You are eternally a part of the Supreme Soul, Kṛṣṇa. By your good fortune, as a result of previous pious activities, you have attained a human birth in the land of India.

Nowadays people think that to be born in America is most fortunate. If given the opportunity, nearly all young Indians would go to America, it being considered the most advanced country in the world. But for spiritual advancement, India is the best. Human life is extremely valuable, being attained only after many births. Humans can inquire about God; animals cannot. Having obtained a human birth, we should at least be thoughtful. Especially the young and bright should apply their intellect to inquire, "Who am I? Where have I come from? What is the meaning of life? What happens after death? What is the highest truth? Who is God, and what is my relationship with Him?" Only if we ask such questions do we give real purpose to our human life.

Human birth in India is especially precious, for India's very atmosphere and culture naturally facilitate spiritual progress. Generally, only persons who have executed pious activities in previous lives are born here, and thus even those from non-Hindu families can avail of the spiritual advantage of having taken birth in India.

Anyone who impartially studies the Vedic message, especially the devotional teachings of Vaiṣṇava *ācāryas*, must conclude—as have so many Westerners also—that the religious traditions of the world find their source and perfection in Vaiṣṇavism, or Kṛṣṇa consciousness. Kṛṣṇa consciousness is non-sectarian in the true sense of the term, for it transcends such designations as Hindu or non-Hindu. The *ātmā* is neither Hindu nor non-Hindu but an eternal particle of God. Consequently, Indians born in non-Hindu families should not consider Kṛṣṇa consciousness merely another sectarian faith. True Kṛṣṇa consciousness is not ordinary religion. It is a scientific education in the highest values of self-surrender to the Supreme Personality of Godhead. Those who reject Kṛṣṇa consciousness out of small-minded sectarianism deny themselves the opportunity for the topmost spiritual fulfilment.

Therefore we again appeal to all Indians—especially the young and inquisitive—not to be fooled by the glittering fantasy of *māyā*. Human life is meant not for decorating the body or cruising around on a motorbike, nor for merely acquiring a comfortable home, nice spouse, and so-called good job. It is meant for understanding God. You were born in the land of the greatest culture. That Vedic culture, based on the dynamic quest for love of God, is eternal, universally applicable, and supremely pure. Its essence cannot be at all polluted. But having been misrepresented by innumerable cheaters, your original culture (*sanātana-dharma*) is now passing as mundane "Hindu religion."

Temples and priests still remain, but spiritual understanding is meagre. Hinduism today is a mishmash of bogus ideas, false avatars, and questionable gurus. Under the circumstances, it is not surprising that many intelligent people are sceptical of what is now called Hinduism, seeing it as blind sentimentalism and empty ritualism. They also fear that Hindu fundamentalism could plunge the nation into bigotry and repression. Nevertheless, most supposed intellectuals are products of an educational system that has deliberately killed their spiritual intelligence. They are steeped in the "rationalism" of a mistaken, materialistic worldview. Apparently being somewhat embarrassed by India's original religious culture, they find little value in her heritage, except perhaps as a tourist attraction. Modern Indians prefer that India be recognized for scientific and industrial achievements rather than spiritual wisdom.

Yet those who are intelligent enough to exercise doubt should also discern that a good thing presented badly is not necessarily bad. The real heritage of Vedic India is not blameworthy, but rather is a vast, comprehensive tradition that offers a zestful, meaningful, and intellectually satisfying way to know oneself as *ātmā* and thereby experience the highest happiness and truth. Although from an ancient past, that wisdom is eternally relevant. Indeed, it is followed even today, in one form or another, by millions, including an increasing number of non-Indians all over the world—which indicates that the spiritual message of India has not been invalidated by her presently weak cultural condition. That the Vedic teachings have been distorted for personal gain does not alter their timeless truths.

Real knowledge never changes. The knowledge of the Vedas is unchangeable because it is based on the absolute truth. Untruths propagated in the name of truth cannot change the absolute truth. Five thousand years ago, that truth was summarized by Lord Kṛṣṇa in *Bhagavad-gītā*, the essence of the Vedas. That we now have TVs, automobiles, and computers does not diminish the *Gītā's* relevance. It is as fresh and alive today as ever before. Those whose intelligence has not been dulled by gross materialism can appreciate the *Gītā's* message. Others cannot.

In *Bhagavad-gītā* Kṛṣṇa's first instructions tell us who we are and what is our position in the universe. In one verse (2.13), He gives us more factual information about reality than is taught in all the schools and universities of the world:

dehino 'smin yathā dehe
kaumāraṁ yauvanaṁ jarā
tathā dehāntara prāptir
dhīras tatra na muhyati

> As the embodied soul continuously passes, in this body, from boyhood to youth to old age, the soul similarly passes into another body at death. A sober person is not bewildered by such a change.

These are the ABCs of spiritual knowledge. Kṛṣṇa explains that we are not these bodies, but the *ātmā* within the body. The body continually changes, and its final change—death—entails the soul's leaving its old body and taking a new one.

The body is *vināśi:* it must be destroyed. But we, who are the *ātmā* within our body, are *avināśi,* indestructible. Under the influence of *māyā,* we are trapped in material bodies. We transmigrate from body to body, in birth after birth in the material world, and despite all endeavours we never attain peace or happiness. In *Bhagavad-gītā* (8.14) Kṛṣṇa describes this world as *duḥkālayam aśāśvatam,* a place of misery wherein repeated birth and death take place. Despite today's machines and technology, the fact remains: material existence is miserable. Therefore we should try to understand our actual spiritual position.

In *Bhagavad-gītā,* Kṛṣṇa explains how the *ātmā* entangled in *māyā* may become disentangled. He describes reincarnation, karma, the material and spiritual worlds, the demigods, and much more. Ultimately, He reveals Himself as the Supreme Personality of Godhead. *Bhagavad-gītā* is a summary of all transcendental knowledge. Although brief, it is complete and perfect. It teaches all that is explained in other scriptures of the world and also reveals truths not found elsewhere.

But so unfortunate are the youth of modern India that, in the land where *Bhagavad-gītā* was spoken, they are not taught the invaluable and essential lessons of *Bhagavad-gītā. Bhagavad-gītā* is studied and respected throughout the world, but nowadays Indians are too "advanced" and "modern" to want to know what it teaches. What a deplorable condition this great land of spiritual culture has degraded into! Innumerable youth pore over sexy magazines, but hardly a few have even once read *Bhagavad-gītā.*

Of course, despite all social pressures, many young Indians do have at least some interest in higher matters. They would do well to take a break from their pressurized life and study *Bhagavad-gītā,* to understand what direction their life is taking. In *Bhagavad-gītā* Lord Kṛṣṇa describes:

> Fearlessness, purification of one's existence, cultivation of spiritual knowledge, charity,

> self-control, performance of sacrifice, study of the Vedas, austerity, simplicity, nonviolence, truthfulness, freedom from anger, renunciation, tranquillity, aversion to faultfinding, compassion for all living entities, freedom from covetousness, gentleness, modesty, steady determination, vigour, forgiveness, fortitude, cleanliness, and freedom from envy and from the passion for honour—these transcendental qualities belong to godly men endowed with divine nature.
>
> Pride, arrogance, conceit, anger, harshness, and ignorance—these qualities belong to those of demoniac nature. The transcendental qualities are conducive to liberation, whereas the demoniac qualities make for bondage. (*Gītā* 16.1–5)

Lord Kṛṣṇa also states:

> My dear Arjuna, how have these impurities come upon you? They are not at all befitting one who knows the value of life. They lead not to higher planets, but to infamy. Do not yield to this degrading impotence. It does not become you. Give up such petty weakness of heart and arise, O chastiser of the enemy! (*Gītā* 2.2–3)

Those who want to be godly should approach a bona fide guru, one who teaches and acts exactly according to *Bhagavad-gītā* as it is (not as he imagines it to be). Such inquisitive persons must beware of cheaters posing as spiritual teachers. A real guru clearly establishes that there is God, that He is a person, that His name is Kṛṣṇa, and that we can revive our loving relationship with Him and become happy forever by chanting His names, especially the *mahā-mantra:* Hare Kṛṣṇa, Hare Kṛṣṇa, Kṛṣṇa Kṛṣṇa, Hare Hare/ Hare Rāma, Hare Rāma, Rāma Rāma, Hare Hare.

Those who think spiritual life to be old-fashioned, boring, or impossibly austere should examine Kṛṣṇa consciousness. Even young people who like fun and fast living will be surprised to find in the Kṛṣṇa consciousness movement a tradition that is ancient yet simultaneously modern and alive—the genuine Vedic knowledge and culture being practiced in the modern age, fully relevant to today's world. If it were simply dogmatic rituals, how could it appeal to the intellectual youth of the West?

Kṛṣṇa consciousness is so practical that anyone can adopt it.* All over the world today, businessmen, students, housewives, farmers, lawyers, doctors, and others practice Kṛṣṇa consciousness alongside their worldly duties. Nonetheless, many young people who want to take up Kṛṣṇa consciousness fear that they will

* For practical guidance on how to be Kṛṣṇa conscious in daily life, see: Bhakti Vikāsa Swami, *A Beginner's Guide to Kṛṣṇa Consciousness* (Mumbai: Bhaktivedanta Book Trust, 1997).

be criticized by others. Our message to them: Don't be afraid! Don't worry about the taunts of foolish people! You have your duty to Kṛṣṇa. He will help you. Even if the whole world were against you (which it never will be), with Kṛṣṇa on your side, what is there to fear? Those who remain strong in their determination to practice Kṛṣṇa consciousness, come what may, will gradually win the respect of others.

Granted, not everyone can just drop everything and radically alter his lifestyle. But anyone, under any circumstance, can take up Kṛṣṇa consciousness at some level. The process is simple. We merely have to welcome Lord Kṛṣṇa into our heart, chant His holy names, and follow His instructions as given in *Bhagavad-gītā As It Is.** All the same, it is wanted that many young people come forward to join this preaching mission full time. Those who are ready to dedicate their life to Kṛṣṇa should actually do so.

Kṛṣṇa consciousness is all-auspicious and opens up an entirely new world of transcendental experience. Especially young people—all over the world—are accepting Kṛṣṇa consciousness as the ultimate solution to all problems. In India too, many educated youth have recognized the value of the Kṛṣṇa consciousness movement and have adopted it with all earnestness.

* By far the world's widest read commentary on this great classic, *Bhagavad-gītā As It Is*, by His Divine Grace A.C. Bhaktivedanta Swami Prabhupāda, is a "must-read" for every educated Indian.

Those who are more serious about Kṛṣṇa consciousness, have a strong sense of adventure, or are determined to make the best use of their valuable human birth should dedicate their life for the highest cause: teaching others how to get free from repeated birth and death.

Everyone is distressed because of not knowing Kṛṣṇa. They need to learn about Him. There are unlimited opportunities for preaching Kṛṣṇa's message. Śrī Caitanya Mahāprabhu particularly wanted Indians to spread Kṛṣṇa consciousness. And Śrīla Prabhupāda repeatedly stressed that educated young Indians should be trained in Kṛṣṇa consciousness and then preach throughout the world.

Wherever the preachers of Kṛṣṇa consciousness go, they meet many people eager to learn about Kṛṣṇa. Westerners often ask, "How is it that although we have all the comforts of push-button technology, we are still dissatisfied? But you Kṛṣṇa devotees live simply and just by chanting Hare Kṛṣṇa become so bright-faced and happy. You devotees are from America, India, Russia, Africa, Japan—from all countries of the world—yet you all work together. How is it possible? What is your secret?"

Many people want to know about Kṛṣṇa. But those of wicked nature oppose the Kṛṣṇa consciousness movement. Devotees have to face the challenges of atheists, demons, and rascals in the garb of scientists, scholars, philosophers, religionists, politicians, and so on. The youth of India should come forward and join this great battle to establish dharma in the age of adharma. As Kṛṣṇa states in *Bhagavad-gītā* (4.42), "The doubts that have arisen in your heart out of ignorance should be slashed by the weapon of knowledge. Armed with yoga, stand and fight."

The world is waiting. The era of change is not yet over. Whatever changes have taken place thus far will seem insignificant compared to the great cultural revolution ahead. People are now asking, "What actual benefit has this industrial civilization given us? In the pursuit of materialism, are we not selling our souls? Is there more to life than working hard for little gain?" The world is looking to India for spiritual knowledge.

Unfortunately, India's good name is ever being spoiled by cheating swamis who go overseas, talk all nonsense, and take people's money. But if sincere Indians preach *Bhagavad-gītā* as it is, gradually the world will gratefully accept it. By spreading the real message of *Bhagavad-gītā*, Indians can do the greatest service to themselves, their country, and mankind. India can lead the world—not by politics, technology, or military dominion, but by spiritual strength. This is Caitanya Mahāprabhu's mission. When Indians have the best knowledge, why should they give anything less? Why cheat people in the name of religion? Give people the real thing: Kṛṣṇa consciousness. The world will be benefited. India will be glorified.

So come forward, young men and women. ISKCON offers a practical process of *bhakti* suitable for the modern age yet in no way compromising the purity of genuine Vedic culture. Join ISKCON and prepare yourself for a glorious future. Senior devotees of ISKCON, those experienced in the preaching field, are trained to guide new members in practicing and propagating Kṛṣṇa consciousness. Serious candidates will receive a full education, both theoretical and practical, in all aspects of this sublime science.

Come live a glorious and happy life and do the greatest good to others. Don't live like an animal—simply eating, sleeping, copulating, and fighting. Don't degrade yourself in the name of modern advancement. If you really want to be progressive and advanced, join the Kṛṣṇa consciousness movement. Don't wait until you are old and worn out. Now is the time. Your fresh youthfulness, adventurous spirit, inquisitiveness, and idealism will be perfectly fulfilled in Kṛṣṇa consciousness. Take to Kṛṣṇa consciousness now—for your own good and for the good of others.

The opportunity is here. Now it's simply up to you to take it.

Śrīla Prabhupāda On India

Quotations from Śrīla Prabhupāda's books, lectures, conversations, and letters

Compiled, edited, and commented on by

Bhakti Vikāsa Swami

Caitanya Mahāprabhu's Mission

bhārata-bhūmite-haila manuṣya-janma yāra
janma sārthaka kari' kara para-upakāra

TRANSLATION

One who has taken his birth as a human being in the land of India (Bhārata-varṣa) should make his life successful and work for the benefit of all other people.

PURPORT

The magnanimity of Lord Caitanya Mahāprabhu is expressed in this very important verse. Although He was born in Bengal, and Bengalis therefore have a special duty toward Him, Śrī Caitanya Mahāprabhu is addressing not only Bengalis but all the inhabitants of India. It is in the land of India that actual human civilization can be developed.

Human life is especially meant for God realization, as stated in the *Vedānta-sūtra* (*athāto brahma-jijñāsā*). Anyone who takes birth in the land of India [Bhārata-varṣa] has the special privilege of being able to take advantage of the instruction and guidance of the Vedic civilization. He automatically receives the basic principles of spiritual life, for 99.9% of the Indian people, even simple village farmers and others who are neither educated nor sophisticated, believe in the transmigration of the soul, believe in past and future lives, believe in God, and naturally want to worship the Supreme Personality of Godhead or His representative. These ideas are the natural inheritance of a person born in India. India has many holy places of pilgrimage—such as Gayā, Benares, Mathurā, Prayāga, Vṛndāvana, Hardwar, Rāmeśvaram, and Jagannātha Purī—and people still go there by the hundreds and thousands. Although the present leaders of India are influencing the people not to believe in God, not to believe in a next life, and not to believe in a distinction between pious and impious life, and they are teaching them how to drink wine, eat meat, and become supposedly civilized, people are nevertheless afraid of the four activities of sinful life, namely illicit sex, meat-eating, intoxication, and gambling, and whenever there is a religious festival they gather together by the thousands. We have actual experience of this. Whenever the Kṛṣṇa consciousness movement holds a *saṅkīrtana* festival in a big city like Calcutta, Bombay, Madras, Ahmedabad, or Hyderabad, thousands of people come to hear. Sometimes we speak in English, but even though most people do not understand English, they nevertheless come to hear us. Even when imitation incarnations of Godhead speak, people gather in thousands, for everyone who is born in the land of India has a natural spiritual inclination and is taught the basic principles of spiritual life; they merely need to be a little more educated in the Vedic principles. Therefore Śrī Caitanya Mahāprabhu said, *janma sārthaka kari' kara para-upakāra*: "If an Indian is educated in the Vedic principles, he is able to perform the most beneficial welfare activity for the entire world."[1]

Every Indian is a devotee. That is the privilege of taking birth in India. Naturally he is a devotee, and if he takes a little education, takes advantage of the Vedic instructions, then his life is successful. In the *śāstra* it is said even the demigods desire to take birth in India because of the facility here. The land is so sanctified that anyone who takes birth here is born sanctified. Now, if he takes further advantage of the Vedic knowledge, then his life becomes successful. Therefore Caitanya Mahāprabhu's mission is that anyone who has taken birth in India should make his life successful, and then preach this knowledge to the outside world. The exact words are:

bhārata-bhūmite-haila manuṣya-janma yāra
janma sārthaka kari' kara para-upakāra

Outside India they are in darkness. So it is the duty of the Indian to make his life perfect and spread this spiritual knowledge to the outside world. That is real welfare activity for the human society. That we are trying to do. Unfortunately, they have not taken very seriously what glorious activities we are doing for India. They do not understand.[2]

Epoch-making History

In other countries there is no civilization. In India there is civilization. Just you become civilized and distribute this knowledge. This is Caitanya Mahāprabhu's preaching. The ocean of mercy was blocked. Let it be opened and distributed throughout the world. So work vigorously. This is epoch-making history, how real culture is being distributed for the benefit of the whole human society.[3]

The Glories of Bhārata-varṣa

India Is the Best Country

India is the best country—there is no doubt. Even these American boys say India is the best. *Puṇya-bhūmi.* For religion and other studies of life, India. These Western boys do not come to India to learn so-called science. They have enough in their own country. They do not come to learn how to manufacture airplanes. There is no need for technology. It is simply bogus. Live simply, save time, and understand your relationship with God—that is India. This is Vedic civilization. India is based on these principles. India is especially meant for understanding God.[4]

India Is the Best Place for Spiritual Life

According to Vedic civilization, the holy places of pilgrimage are considered most sacred, and there are still hundreds and thousands of holy places like Jagannātha Purī, Vṛndāvana, Hardwar, Rāmeśvaram, Prayāga, and Mathurā. India is the place for worshiping, or for cultivating spiritual life. The Kṛṣṇa consciousness movement invites everyone from all over the world, without discrimination as to caste or creed, to come to its centres and cultivate spiritual life perfectly.[5]

Everyone who happens to take his birth in India is a potential benefactor of others, because it is on

Indian soil alone that the culture of transcendental knowledge has been most elaborately presented, from ancient times to the present. The saints and sages of Bhārata-varṣa, as India has long been known, never tried to cultivate or satisfy artificially the needs of the body and the mind exclusively; they always cultured the transcendental spirit soul, which is above the material body and mind. And even now, the saints and sages continue to do so, in spite of all difficulties.[6]

Birth in India Is Special

The learned sages inform us that one takes his birth in India, the holy land of Bhārata-varṣa, after the gradual process of evolution through 8,400,000 species of life, including 900,000 aquatic species, 2,000,000 nonmoving species such as vegetables and hills, 1,100,000 germ and insect species, 1,000,000 bird species, 3,000,000 lower-animal species, and 400,000 human species. The living spirit transmigrates from one species of life to another, and he is moving in that way for millions and millions of years within the hollow of the great universe.[7]

The special feature of a birth in India is that a person born in India becomes automatically God conscious. In every part of India, and especially in the holy places of pilgrimage, even an ordinary, uneducated man is inclined toward Kṛṣṇa consciousness, and as soon as he sees a Kṛṣṇa conscious person he offers obeisances. India has many sacred rivers like the Ganges, Yamunā, Narmadā, Kāverī, and Kṛṣṇā, and simply by bathing in these rivers people are liberated and become Kṛṣṇa conscious.[8]

A short life in the land of Bhārata-varṣa is preferable to a life achieved in Brahma-loka for millions and billions of years, because even if one is elevated to Brahma-loka he must return to repeated birth and death. Although life in Bhārata-varṣa, in a lower planetary system, is very short, one who lives there can elevate himself to full Kṛṣṇa consciousness and achieve the highest perfection, even in this short life, by fully surrendering unto the lotus feet of the Lord. Thus one attains Vaikuṇṭha-loka, where there is neither anxiety nor repeated birth in a material body.[9]

Even the Demigods Desire Birth in India

In the *Kūrma Purāṇa* there is this statement about the desires of the demigods:

anadhikāriṇo devāḥ
svarga-sthā bhāratodbhavam
vāñchanty ātma-vimokṣārtha-
mudrekārthe 'dhikāriṇaḥ

Although the demigods are situated in exalted positions in the heavenly planets, they nevertheless desire to descend to the land of Bhārata-varṣa on the planet earth. This indicates that even the demigods are unfit to reside in Bhārata-varṣa. Therefore, if persons already born in Bhārata-varṣa live like cats and dogs, not taking full advantage of their birth in this land, they are certainly unfortunate.[10]

Every Indian Is Kṛṣṇa Conscious

Actually, every Indian is Kṛṣṇa conscious. Sometimes in foreign countries they ask me, "How many Kṛṣṇa conscious people are there in India?" And [I tell them,] "Cent percent, all—even Muslims, what to speak of the Hindus."[11]

Practically the whole population of India is dedicated to spiritual life. Anyone who has taken birth in India has got a natural inheritance of spiritual life. Unfortunately, at the present moment the leaders are under the wrong impression that because India is too much spiritually inclined, its material advancement has been checked. But material advancement does not become hampered by spiritual knowledge. That is a wrong impression. Rather, if you become spiritually advanced, your material necessities will be very nicely adjusted.[12]

Although there is propaganda in India to get people to forget Kṛṣṇa consciousness, it is not possible for them to forget, because Kṛṣṇa Himself appeared there.[13]

India Once Ruled the World

It is clear that the kings of India once ruled all the world and that their culture was Vedic.[14]

More than five thousand years ago, while Saint Vidura was travelling the earth as a pilgrim, India was known as Bhārata-varṣa, as it is known even today. The history of the world cannot give any systematic account for more than three thousand years into the past, but before that the whole world was under the flag and military strength of Mahārāja Yudhiṣṭhira, who was the emperor of the world. At present there are hundreds and thousands of flags flapping in the United Nations, but during the time of Vidura there was, by the grace of Ajita, Lord Kṛṣṇa, only one flag. The nations of the world are very eager to again have one state under one flag, but for this they must seek the favour of Lord Kṛṣṇa, who alone can help us become one worldwide nation.[15]

Outsiders Are Accepting Kṛṣṇa Consciousness

It is a glory for us that people in other countries, outside India, are accepting this cult of Kṛṣṇa consciousness.[16]

The Land of Religion

This is the land of religion. It is admitted by other parts of the world. Columbus was searching after

India for trade, even hundreds of years ago. People are coming to India for knowledge, philosophy, trade, and money. Why did the Britishers come? For money. India was exploited for thousands of years and the standard of civilization deteriorated. Still, India's position is unique, even in this fallen condition. Now people are degraded from their previous, high standard, both spiritually and materially. Still, they have their feelings for religion. It is still going on.[17]

There are millions and billions of followers of Kṛṣṇa in India. Not only ordinary followers—also many great stalwarts, educationists, and saintly persons like Śaṅkarācārya, Madhvācārya, Rāmānujācārya, Lord Caitanya, and other great educated and learned scholars, have accepted Kṛṣṇa. There are so many others also. And there are millions and millions of temples of Kṛṣṇa. They are being worshipped by millions and billions of devotees still. Still, if you go to some Kṛṣṇa temple in South India, you'll find thousands of thousands of people always assembled. Whenever you go in that Jaipur temple, within the king's palace, you'll find at least one thousand men assembled. If you go to Jagannātha Purī, you'll find at least two thousand men, daily coming and going. If you go to Vṛndāvana, you'll find at least five thousand men, daily coming and going. In Vṛndāvana itself there are five thousand temples. Out of that only seven or eight are very big. In other words, each and every house is a Kṛṣṇa temple. Somebody asked me, "How many Kṛṣṇa conscious people are there in India?" At least ninety percent of the Hindus are Kṛṣṇa conscious.[18]

India's Present Condition

Comment: India is the land of Kṛṣṇa and Rāma, of Bhagavad-gītā, *of Gaṅgā, of sages and rishis—the land of religion and culture. Even materially, originally India was so rich that the Moguls and Europeans, coming from a great distance with much difficulty, fought with each other for the opportunity to exploit her. Today India still has plentiful natural resources, and with her vast pool of highly educated people, recently has become much modernized and economically progressive. Nevertheless, most Indians still live below the poverty line, with no hope of ever rising above it. India's cities are overcrowded, disordered, and filthy. Lying, cheating, corruption, exploitation, violence, and murder are part of everyday life. People are full of anxiety. No one trusts anyone else. No one is happy.*

Once famous for their devotion to God, Indians now prefer to worship unchaste women, fools, rascals, and paper currency. In traditional Indian civilization, ladies were respected and glorified for their chastity. Now women known as film heroines flirt before millions and vulgarly expose their body to all. Indian womanhood has been demeaned by these females of slight virtue who are nonetheless adored like goddesses.

The fools in India are many, among whom sports stars are prominent. The whole country is crazy about cricket—really crazy—getting so excited about someone throwing a ball and someone else hitting it with a piece of wood. It is an event of monumental meaninglessness that only by mental concoction is given such importance. Factually, the outcome of the game makes no essential difference to anyone or anything, except within the minds of those stupid enough to take it seriously.

Indian rascals are also numerous. Politicians are widely honoured even though everyone knows that almost all of them are corrupt, self-interested cheaters and liars. Atheistic scientists are also big rascals. Nowadays people question what Kṛṣṇa says in the Bhagavad-gītā *but implicitly accept the scientists' words, even though scientists talk all nonsense (such as, "Life is a product of matter"), regularly contradict each other, and have been proved wrong on innumerable occasions. Another class of* mahā-*rascals are the petty magicians who dare call themselves God.*

For most Indians today, even all these "gods" are not as important as the paper god. Everyone has dedicated himself—body, mind, and soul—to the acquisition of money.

Of course, faith in Kṛṣṇa and Rāma has not been completely abandoned. A "Rāma revival" is now on, although some claim it to be more political than spiritual. Temple-going is on the increase. But everyone goes for material benedictions: "I need money," "Help me pass my exams," "Give me this," "Give me that." No one is interested to love God for His own sake.

Even among those who consider themself pious, most are not very serious about religion. Among their personal interests, religion ranks below family, business, TV, sports, cinema, and politics. Even some pious-minded Indians, under the influence of modern trends, now think that sinful activities such as eating meat, fish, and eggs, taking alcohol, tobacco, and other intoxicants, or performing extra-marital sex or abortion are not so bad, quite normal, or even proper.

This is the position of puṇya-bhūmi *today. How did this great country fall into such a deplorable state? In this and the next section, Śrīla Prabhupāda analyzes India's present condition and the multiple causes of her decline.*

The time is very bad at the present moment everywhere, especially in India. Of course, India's original culture is all right. But unfortunately, our modern leaders are killing the original culture. They want to introduce Western culture. Now openly there are beef shops and wine shops. What can be done? It is Kali-yuga. But those who are intelligent should take to this Kṛṣṇa consciousness movement and make their human life successful.[19]

Every living entity has got the tendency for sex life, meat-eating, and liquor. The country where these things are indulged in without restriction is called the country of the *asuras* (demons). That is especially in the Western countries, and now we have also learned.

In India, for both Hindus and Muslims, drinking was a sin, but now liquor is easily available, and at every door there is a meat shop. There was time when all in India were *devatās* (godly). Now we are imitating the *asuras*.[20]

Now in India also, where some Vedic principles were still glowing, that is also being finished.

pravṛttiṁ ca nivṛttiṁ ca
janā na vidur āsurāḥ
na śaucaṁ nāpi cācāro
na satyaṁ teṣu vidyate

> Those who are demoniac do not know what is to be done and what is not to be done. Neither cleanliness, nor proper behaviour, nor truth are found in them. (*Gītā* 16.7)

They are learning from the Westerners how to remain unclean, how to eat meat, how to drink wine, and so on. And they do not know what is truthfulness. In other words, everyone is a liar.[21]

In India, which was once the land of religion and brahminical culture, things have deteriorated to such an extent that a man in a higher caste is recognized simply by putting a piece of thread on the body as a sign of sanctity. The so-called swamis are cheating the public because the public also want to be cheated by cheap methods of self-realization. They are practicing so-called yoga performances for reducing fat and keeping the body fit for sense gratification. If one has insufficient money, it is very hard for him to get justice from the court. And if anyone can simply bluff by so-called advancement of knowledge, he is offered the doctorate degree. If a man is poor, he is at once accepted as uncivilized. If a man is falsely proud, he is accepted as civilized.[22]

"Modern" people in India are all rascals.[23]

After losing our own culture, we have become a set of fools. We have become so lowest of mankind and *mūḍha* (fool) and full of sinful activities that we cannot understand what Kṛṣṇa says.[24]

When a person forgets his position as an eternal servant of Kṛṣṇa, he commits many sinful activities, but one who maintains his position as an eternal servant of Kṛṣṇa cannot deviate from the path of morality, religion, and ethics. At the present, people all over the world, *especially in India,* have forgotten their relationship with the Supreme Personality of Godhead and His eternal servants. Therefore the principles of morality, religion, and ethics have almost disappeared. This situation is most unprofitable for human society. Therefore everyone should try to accept Kṛṣṇa consciousness and follow the principles of Śrī Caitanya Mahāprabhu.[25]

It was customary for members of the three higher classes, namely the *brāhmaṇas, kṣatriyas,* and *vaiśyas,* to worship the *śālagrāma-śilā* or a small deity of Rādhā-Kṛṣṇa or Sītā-Rāma in each and every home. This made everything auspicious. But now they have given up deity worship. Men have become modernized and are consequently indulging in all sorts of sinful activities, and therefore they are extremely unhappy.[26]

When we consider the past condition of the agriculturalist in the village, we can see how opulent he was, simply because of agricultural produce and protection of cows. At the present, however, agriculture having been neglected and cow protection given up, the agriculturalist is suffering pitiably and is dressed in a niggardly torn cloth. This is the distinction between the India of history and the India of the present day. By the atrocious activities of *ugra-karma*, how we are killing the opportunity of human civilization!* [27]

In the educational system, there is no *Bhagavad-gītā*. How unfortunate! One Indian girl in Berkeley University asked me, "Swamiji, what is God?" Just see. She's Indian, from where God, Rāmacandra or Kṛṣṇa, takes birth, and she is now materially advanced. Now she is asking "What is God?" That is our position. From the land where God comes, an advanced student is asking "What is God?" That is our advancement.[28]

In India Kṛṣṇa comes, in India Lord Rāmacandra comes. But they have now taken it very cheaply. Rascals and fools and rogues are claiming that "I am Kṛṣṇa." They are accepted because India has fallen.

---

* *Ugra-karma*—unnecessary, soul-killing, gross hard work, such as in factories, mines, etc.

Because there is no brahminical culture, they cannot understand that those who claim to be Kṛṣṇa are fools and rascals. Is Kṛṣṇa so cheap? No. Instead of accepting Kṛṣṇa, we are accepting some imitation, some rogue, as Kṛṣṇa. This is our misfortune.[29]

What is the position of India? Nobody cares for India. Wherever I go, they say, "Oh, India? That's a poverty-stricken country." That is your good name. Because your administrators are going, "Give me this," "Give me that," "Give me money," "Give me weapons so we can be saved from the slapping of Pakistan"—a begging business. India's position is not very glorious outside India. You may be puffed up that you have become independent. But everyone is anxious to have your spiritual culture, everyone. They know that "if you want to know about spiritual culture and religion, you must go to India."[30]

In India, we have to fight a little. There are so many atheists. But the mass of people are all right.[31]

Causes of India's Downfall

The Influence of Kali-yuga

Even fifty years ago, the social structure of all Indians was so arranged that they would not read any literature that was not connected with the activities of the Lord. They would not play any drama not connected with the Lord. They would not organize a fair or ceremony not connected with the Lord. Therefore even the common man in the village would talk about *Rāmāyaṇa* and *Mahābhārata*, *Gītā* and *Bhāgavatam*, even from his very childhood. But by the influence of the Age of Kali, they have been dragged to the civilization of the dogs and hogs, labouring for bread without any sense of transcendental knowledge.[32]

Imitating the West

Comment: The world seems to be going back to front. At a time when many Westerners are looking to India for enlightenment, Indians are becoming increasingly enamoured by the Western way of life, with all its shallowness and paucity of moral values. Yet Indians' attempts to Westernize themselves have not been very successful. For Westerners, indulgence in degraded sense enjoyment comes naturally, whereas Indians are simply not meant for grossly sinful living. Despite all their attempts, Indians are not and cannot be the same as

Westerners, for their spiritually based culture and mental outlook are quite different from that of Westerners. Suffering from a massive (yet unfounded!) inferiority complex, they have opted for wholesale imitation.

Indians simply copy everything Western without considering whether it is appropriate for them or not. For instance, pants and shirts with shoes and socks may be suitable for the cold climes of the West, but hardly so in the sweltering heat of India. Yet modern Indian men prefer the discomfort of unnatural Western dress to the embarrassment of dhoti and kurta.

Indians blindly follow the West, without considering that for all its much advertized glamour and "good life," the West is plagued with extremely severe social problems, including rampant divorce, suicide, sexual perversion, violence, crime, alcoholism, and drug addiction. Although modern so-called civilization may look good on TV, in reality it is nasty, unhappy, hollow, and devoid of higher values. It is a disaster, and getting worse. Westerners have proved themselves to be materially competent, but spiritually they are nowhere. Therefore thoughtful Westerners are looking to India to help restore the balance between material and spiritual.

Meanwhile, Indians continue to mimic Western ideas. But they should know that along with the excitement and apparent enjoyment of Western life comes a whole package of moral decrepitude. Indian society has enough problems of its own without importing those of the West.

Traditionally, Indians were taught to accept whatever position they were in to be the grace of God and to thus be satisfied in any condition of life. But modern consumer society teaches one to never be satisfied, even if he has millions of dollars, but to always hanker for more. Which is better: to be happy even in difficulty, or discontent in the midst of plenty?

Why are Indians so eager to degrade themselves in the name of modernization? Why have they become their own worst enemy? Do they not consider what a great treasure they are neglecting? The Westerners who came to India for looting did quite a thorough job, but they didn't get the greatest treasure of India—her profound spiritual culture—until Śrīla Prabhupāda came and gave it to them. Here is what Śrīla Prabhupāda has to say about the imitation process:

Indians? They are imitating this material civilization. Horrible.[33]

Anyone who has taken birth in India can fulfil the mission of human life. They have got a very good asset. But unfortunately they have rejected it. They are now enamoured by the glamour of material civilization. Looking to Europe and America, they want skyscraper buildings and industry, and want to be happy in that way. But actually, that is not the way. That is, rather, misleading. The more we advance this material way of life, the more we are away from spiritual life. Human life is meant for spiritual realization. Nothing more.[34]

Our modern Indian leaders are simply imitators of the Westerners. Western people, Western civilization, has become the father and mother of India.[35]

The state of India should better follow the example of Mahārāja Parīkṣit, the ideal executive head, than to imitate other materialistic states which have no idea of the kingdom of Godhead, the ultimate goal of human life. Deterioration of the ideals of Indian civilization has brought about the deterioration of civic life, not only in India but also abroad.[36]

Comment: India's neglect of her spiritual heritage has resulted not only in her own decline. The present chaotic condition in the world could have been avoided had Indians taken up their duty to spread Kṛṣṇa consciousness all over the world.

Indians are meant for *paropakāra* (welfare activities for others), because outside India they are in darkness. But unfortunately, Indians are now imitating the Western kind of life. It is very regrettable.[37]

Comment: Śrīla Prabhupāda once told the story of a brāhmaṇa *who, being very hungry and finding no other means, begged food from the house of a Muslim. The Muslim fed him, but when the* brāhmaṇa *asked for more, his host regretfully replied that he had nothing extra to give. "Oh," lamented the* brāhmaṇa, *"I have lost my caste but am still hungry!" Similarly, India, being hungry for Western-style achievements, has given up her own culture yet has not been able to develop as opulently as the Western countries. Therefore she is like the* brāhmaṇa *who lost his caste but was still hungry.*

Misleadership

Indians are trained by culture and birth. The land of Bhārata-varṣa is *puṇya-bhūmi.* Still, at Kumbha-melā many millions of people come to take bath in the Ganges, because it is pious. Spiritual fluid flows through the veins of Indians. Unfortunately, the leaders are misguiding them and they are becoming atheists. It is a very regrettable situation.[38]

Every Indian has got a great opportunity because this is the land of religion, the land of spiritual knowledge. But they are being taught, "Throw away these books." India is now in such an unfortunate condition. They are recommending wholesale cow slaughter in India, to make business. Unfortunately we have to be governed by such rascals.[39]

It has been a long process how the Indians, especially educated Indians, have become victimized by the slowly deteriorating position of Indian culture. There is no use tracing out the history, but generally we have lost our own culture, and our leaders are not very serious to revive it. Still the mass of people, being not very much advanced in education, stick to the Indian culture. For example, lakhs of people still visit Jagannātha Purī during the Rathayātrā festival, lakhs still visit the Kumbha-melā, and lakhs still visit the holy places of India. But there is no encouragement by the leaders.[40]

Being a spiritualistic country, why has India fallen into darkness? Because there is great propaganda by the leaders to curb spiritual culture. Those born in India are understood to have practiced spiritual life in their previous lives. There is great opportunity for spiritual advancement for those born in India. They are naturally inclined. Unfortunately, by force, by propaganda, we are suppressing them. Still, we get experience that when we hold Hare Kṛṣṇa festivals in Calcutta, Bombay, and other places, many thousands of people come—because at heart there is Kṛṣṇa consciousness, but by external force they are being suppressed. It is not natural; it is unnatural. By nature, every Indian is Kṛṣṇa conscious. By artificial means they are being suppressed. This is the misfortune of present-day India.[41]

We do not want to criticize anyone, but sometimes it so happens: big, big scholars, big, big politicians, misguide people. That is the position of India. So many big, big leaders and politicians and so-called swamis and yogis have exploited people by bluffing, and now India's position is neither spiritual nor material. Just like if there are two boats and we place one leg in one boat and the other leg in the other, our position becomes very precarious. So we are like that—neither in this boat nor in that boat. We are learning technology, and the Western countries are always a hundred years ahead of us. We cannot compete. This technology is for *śūdras.*

Technology is not the occupation for the *brāhmaṇas*, *kṣatriyas*, or *vaiśyas*. That is not knowledge. Knowledge means to know God. The Western countries take advancement of knowledge to mean manufacturing big motorcars—that's all. That is also good, but simply for manufacturing motorcars if we forget our real business, God realization, then it is ruinous. Then we become *mūḍhas*.[42]

After many, many births, one is given the opportunity to take birth in this holy land of Bhārata-varṣa. Unfortunately, you are by force making them materialistic. They had the opportunity to take advantage of the contribution of great sages and rishis, to study and to become a successful human being, but by force you are dragging them to this materialistic way of life. This is violence.[43]

At the present moment in India the presidential offices are occupied by many so-called *brāhmaṇas*, but the state maintains slaughterhouses for killing cows and makes propaganda against Vedic civilization. The first principle of Vedic civilization is the avoidance of meat-eating and intoxication. Presently in India, intoxication and meat-eating are encouraged, and the so-called learned *brāhmaṇas* presiding over this state of affairs have certainly become degraded. These so-called *brāhmaṇas* give sanction to slaughterhouses for the sake of a fat salary, and they do not protest these abominable activities. By deprecating the principles of Vedic civilization and supporting cow killing, they are immediately degraded to the platform of *mlecchas* and *yavanas*. A *mleccha* is a meat-eater, and a *yavana* is one who has deviated from Vedic culture. Unfortunately, such *mlecchas* and *yavanas* are in executive power. How then can there be peace and prosperity in the state?[44]

Nowadays people are being taught to drink wine, eat meat, and do whatever they like. So they will go down to animal life. They have no knowledge. The leaders are blind and they are leading other blind men. So it is a very dangerous civilization. In spite of being born in India, in spite of having the privilege of studying *Bhagavad-gītā*, they are not taking advantage of it, and they are being misled like cats and dogs. It is a very regrettable condition. The Kṛṣṇa consciousness movement is the only challenge to this devilish life of the human society. So I request everyone to study this philosophy very carefully and take advantage of it.[45]

We should take advantage of the *śāstras*, Vedic knowledge. It is India's property. Spiritual knowledge was cultivated in India, but because *andhā yathāndhair upanīyamānāḥ* (the blind are leading the blind)—our rascal leaders are leading these *andhās*—they are not interested. They are now interested how to eat meat and drink wine. This is India's very horrible condition. Responsible people should take note of it and try to spread the Kṛṣṇa consciousness movement as far as possible. That will be beneficial for all the people in general and for the preachers also. This is our movement.[46]

Don't Blame the Government

Now there is democracy. The government are the people's men. If we are ourselves fools and rascals, the government will also be a set of fools and rascals. And if you are intelligent, the government will be intelligent. So don't blame the government. You are the government. It is up to you to change; then everything will be all right.[47]

Kṛṣṇa Consciousness Should Have Been Made the State Religion

One of the objects of my missionary activities is to bring to notice of the educated Indian public that devotional service originated in India. Now the leaders of India are deliberately violating all the principles of India's original spiritual culture, in the name of the secular state. When India was divided into Hindustan and Pakistan, there was a good opportunity for the Hindu Indians to follow strictly the principles of *Bhagavad-gītā,* and Kṛṣṇa consciousness should have been declared the state religion.[48]

Spiritual Culture Rejected

When we come to civilized life we should not waste our time like animals. Those who are born in India, Bhārata-bhūmi, are considered the topmost. Therefore Caitanya Mahāprabhu said, *bhārata-bhūmite haila manuṣya-janma yāra/ janma sārthaka kari' kara para-upakāra.* This is Caitanya Mahāprabhu's mission: those who have taken birth in Bhārata-bhūmi should make their life perfect by understanding the Vedic knowledge. The Supreme Lord, Kṛṣṇa, comes here to teach the Vedic knowledge. He left *Bhagavad-gītā*. Then Vyāsadeva developed the idea of Kṛṣṇa consciousness from *Bhagavad-gītā* and *Vedānta-sūtra* into *Śrīmad-Bhāgavatam*. So we have got this advantage, but we are giving it up. The advantage is that we are born in India, and we have got the stock of knowledge left by great sages, and the Supreme Personality of Godhead. But we are not taking advantage of it. How foolish we are becoming by so-called education![49]

Spiritual culture is in India practically rejected. They are convinced that because of spiritual culture we are so much behind materially. That is their full conviction.[50]

Malinterpretation of Scripture

For our guidance Kṛṣṇa has spoken everything in *Bhagavad-gītā*. Unfortunately, so-called scholars and saintly persons have misguided the people by making different interpretations of the divine instruction unnecessarily. That is the cause of the ruination of our culture in India.[51]

This rascaldom [of misinterpreting scripture] has killed the whole spiritual atmosphere of India. They are responsible, these rascal politicians and rascal so-called scholars. If we want the good of the people, these rascals should be disclosed and people should come back to their own culture. Therefore we are presenting *Bhagavad-gītā* as it is.[52]

Those who take Indian philosophy and scripture as mythological are not at all intelligent. They have been described in the *Bhagavad-gītā* (7.15) as "sinful," "rascals," "lowest of mankind," "bereft of all knowledge," and "atheistic."

na māṁ duṣkṛtino mūḍhāḥ
prapadyante narādhamāḥ
māyayāpahṛta-jñānā
āsuraṁ bhāvam āśritāḥ

> Those miscreants who are grossly foolish, who are lowest among mankind, whose knowledge is stolen by illusion, and who partake of the atheistic nature of demons do not surrender unto Me (Kṛṣṇa).

The psychological conception of the so-called Indian philosophers has killed Indian civilization.[53]

They won't believe a word of Kṛṣṇa and they'll say, "I am a student of *Bhagavad-gītā*." In India everyone says, "I have read *Bhagavad-gītā* three hundred times," but he does not know even a word. This should be stopped. If we want to actually advance, we should take every word of *Bhagavad-gītā* and try to apply it in our lives. Then everyone will be happy. That is a fact.[54]

Not Accepting Kṛṣṇa's Supremacy and Authority

That is the difficulty in India. As soon as we say, "Kṛṣṇa is the Supreme Lord. There is no one superior to Kṛṣṇa," others will say, "No, why is this gentleman not superior to Kṛṣṇa?" That is the difficulty. They'll not accept. Their brain is filled with hodgepodge things. Therefore they cannot take to Kṛṣṇa consciousness properly. Of course at heart, in India, everyone feels for Kṛṣṇa, but they have been educated in such a wrong way that they cannot accept Kṛṣṇa as the Supreme. This is the difficulty. Unless you accept that Kṛṣṇa is the Supreme, your education, your knowledge, and everything else is imperfect.[55]

You do not read the *Bhagavad-gītā*. You quote some so-called saint, and another, and another. But Kṛṣṇa is God. The cause of India's misfortune is that you don't accept Kṛṣṇa as the authority. All the great sages—such as Asita, Devala, Vyāsa, and in the present era Rāmānujācārya, Madhvācārya, Nimbārka, Caitanya Mahāprabhu—accept *kṛṣṇas tu bhagavān:* "Kṛṣṇa is the Supreme Personality of Godhead." But you don't follow the *ācāryas*, the authorities, or Kṛṣṇa. You bring some concoction. They have given up the real authority and accepted some foolish man as an authority. Therefore we are presenting *Bhagavad-gītā As It Is*, the supreme authority. *Mattaḥ parataraṁ nānyat kiñcid asti dhanañjaya; ahaṁ sarvasya prabhavo mattaḥ sarvaṁ pravartate* [from *Bhagavad-gītā:* Kṛṣṇa declares that there is no truth superior to Him; He is the source of everything]. Why don't you take this?[56]

Indians Are Becoming Insane

This has spoiled our India's Vedic culture. Everyone has invented their own way, and they have misled the common people. That is the misfortune of modern India. The standard instruction is there in the *Bhagavad-gītā*. They do not care to know it. They want to know about the greatness of Bala Yogi, Sai Baba, this *baba*, that *baba*. They give up the real instruction, *Bhagavad-gītā*, which is accepted by the great *ācāryas*—Rāmānujācārya, Madhvācārya, Nimbārka, Caitanya Mahāprabhu—and which is accepted all over the world. They are not interested to know *Bhagavad-gītā;* they are interested to know about Sai Baba. They give up the real thing and accept the imitation. Just see their misfortune! India is so misguided that it will take some time to come. What will I speak to India? *Bhagavad-gītā. Bhagavad-gītā* was already there, and still is there. But India's misfortune is that they are so neglectful they don't care for it. They'll ask, "Why not this *baba*? Why not that *baba*?" That is the difficulty. They have become "over-intelligent," not actually intelligent. We are preaching that Kṛṣṇa is the Supreme Lord. That is in the *śāstra* and the Vedas, everywhere. But you won't believe it. You'll say, "Why is Kṛṣṇa the Supreme God? Here is another God. And another. And another."

You'll bring hundreds and thousands of "Gods." Certainly I plan to propagate this message in India, but who is going to take it? *Bhagavad-gītā* is already there, but who will take it? They will bring another competition. "Ah, what Hare Kṛṣṇa? We have heard it. We have seen *Bhagavad-gītā*." If you become neglectful, that is the greatest offence. So India is an offender. What I am preaching to others is India's philosophy. But Indians won't take it. Anyone who is sane, sober, and open-minded will agree with what I say. Not only Hindus—we have got so many Muslims also. So unless one is open-minded, sane, and intelligent, one cannot understand. Therefore I say that Indians are becoming insane. By the influence of so many rascals they are becoming insane. Insanity is prevailing all over the world, but not so much as in India—that they are rejecting their own thing. That is the greatest insanity. That has to be rectified.[57]

Impersonalism

Comment: Impersonalism means Māyāvāda (advaita-vāda), the erroneous and offensive idea that God, the Supreme, is not a person, but an all-pervasive essence that we can become one with. This is nothing but a covered form of atheism that tricks people into thinking that they are pious while actually making them deeply envious of Kṛṣṇa. Impersonalism has poisoned India's spiritual life, robbed the vital current of pure devotion, and is the underlying cause of her present godlessness, immorality, and hedonism. For an elaborate discussion of this important subject, see Śrīla Prabhupāda's Teachings of Lord Caitanya.

Impersonalism has killed India's Vedic culture. On account of these impersonalists, Māyāvādīs, the whole of India has become godless. They misinterpret just to mislead people. This is the misfortune of India. Don't be misled by these rascals. Take the real *Bhagavad-gītā*, as it is. Then you'll be benefited.[58]

The British Influence

India is a country of religion. Indians know that spiritual life is more important than material life. That is India. Now they are diverting their attention to the material; otherwise the whole of India is for spiritual life. This material life is brought from the Western countries. These railways, bridges, factories, industries, export and import, and then slaughterhouse, drinking, and prostitution—these are all the British contribution. In India, before that, they did not know these things. The British policy was "If the Indians remain Indian, it will be impossible to govern them. Give them education and condemn everything Indian." There was not a single factory before the British days. The industry idea is completely Western. And tea gardens.[59]

Comment: Even cricket and democracy, now part of Indian life, are imported from the West. They are not part of India's original, spiritual-based heritage.

The British were expert politicians. Their intelligent policy was to kill India's spiritual status. One British politician, Lord McCauley, studied the whole Indian situation. He reported, "If you keep Indians as Indians, you'll never be able to rule over them. They must be trained up to think of their own culture as useless and that Western culture is very good. That impression must be there. Otherwise you cannot rule over them." So the education and everything was going on imperceptibly on this principle. That went on for the last two hundred years. So educated persons lost their culture. The mass of people were not educated. They have not lost their culture, but they don't find any good example by the leaders. They are simply staying somehow or other in their original culture, but there is no encouragement by the leaders. Just like one of India's first post-independence leaders was a complete rascal about Indian culture. He did not think that Indian culture has any value. In his book about "discovering India" he recommended that Indians become Europeanized—industry, the Western way of living and eating, pollution, abortion, and everything.[60]

Government Policy

The government thinks that because Indian people are too much religiously inclined, they have fallen down economically. Therefore these religious sentiments should be stopped completely. It is not encouraged. Here in Vṛndāvana so many pilgrims come from all parts of India, and now from all parts of the world. But Vṛndāvana is deliberately kept in such an unclean state to discourage people from coming here. That is the idea—so that educated, modernized people may not come here. They are introducing industry in the Vṛndāvana area so that the spiritual atmosphere will be killed. The temples are neglected. No question of improvement. The whole idea is not to come here: "Please do not come." They cannot say it directly, but this is the idea going on. This is due to wrong direction of civilization. They do not know the aim of civilization, which is to understand Viṣṇu, the Supreme Personality of Godhead. They are missing the point. They are thinking the motor-tyre civilization, with very nice roads and cars running at eighty miles an hour, is civilization. We should not be misled by such a misconception of civilization. Our aim is different.[61]

Caste Consciousness

Because one happens to take birth in a *brāhmaṇa* family, without any qualification, he claims to become a *brāhmaṇa*. That is the falldown of Vedic civilization in India. A rascal number one claims that he is a *brāhmaṇa*, without any qualification. His qualification is less than that of a *śūdra*.[62]

The idea of Vedic civilization is to gradually elevate everyone to the position of *brāhmaṇa* and

Vaiṣṇava and thus make their life perfect. Not "Keep the *śūdras* or the *mlecchas* in a downtrodden position, and let me advance." No. Everyone should cooperate. Why should the *śūdras* or *mlecchas* and *yavanas* remain as such? Actually, India's falldown is because nobody cared. So many were converted, but the higher castes did not care. "Oh, they have become Muslims. Reject them." Why? Kṛṣṇa says the opposite:

māṁ hi pārtha vyapāśritya
ye 'pi syuḥ pāpa-yonayaḥ
striyo vaiśyās tathā śūdrās
te 'pi yānti parāṁ gatim

Even those of lower birth can be delivered if they take shelter of Me (Kṛṣṇa). (*Gītā* 9.32)

Why were these Muslims neglected? Why were they not turned into Vaiṣṇavas, as we are doing? This is the fault of the leaders. Therefore India is now divided into Pakistan and Hindustan.[63]

Partition

In a country like India, where the population is very big and there is limited land, there must be food scarcity. The British divided India into Pakistan and Hindustan. This artificial partition has caused trouble because Pakistan has taken away all the wheat and rice. All the food grains are on the Pakistan side, and all the industries on the Hindustan side. So they are fighting.

Due to this partition only, India's position is now very crippled.[64]

The Cinema

Perverse sexuality is now very much advertised in the cinema to attract people. Formerly in India it was not so, but gradually they are introducing all this nonsense to make people more lusty. And to become lusty means that they are going to hell.[65]

Comment: Whatever the cinema has done to degrade the Indian public is now being greatly accelerated with the introduction of foreign TV and the internet.

India Should Have Distributed Spiritual Knowledge

They are instructing, "If you want economic development, why go to the church or temple? Just start industry. You'll get money." That propaganda is going on in India. "Forget God and the temples. Just try to imitate America. Become industrialized overnight." But they are not teaching them that in the Western countries, after industrialization, they are producing hippies. That they do not see. They are seeing only one side: "America and the Western countries have become prosperous by industrialization. Let us imitate them." Actually India, after independence, should have distributed this spiritual knowledge. Why should we compete with industrialization? The Westerners also have a demand for spiritual knowledge. So India should have given spiritual knowledge to the Western countries instead of competing with industry.[66]

Fortunately, in India we have got everything, but our modern leaders are neglecting their own thing. They are begging technology from other countries. That is their misfortune. I am singlehandedly trying to present the original Vedic culture. People all over the world are accepting it very happily. India should have tried for this. The government should have known better. Unfortunately, they are all bereft of knowledge of their own culture. There is a Bengali verse: *āpana dhana bilāya diye bhikṣa māge parera kāche* [begging from others after distributing one's own wealth]. They have lost their own culture; now they are begging from other countries.[67]

Knowledge is meant for distribution. Although there is already much scientific knowledge, whenever scientists or philosophers awaken to a particular type of knowledge they try to distribute it throughout the world, for otherwise the knowledge gradually dries up and no one benefits from it. India has the knowledge of *Bhagavad-gītā,* but unfortunately, for some reason or other, this sublime knowledge of the science of God was not distributed throughout the world, although it is meant for all of human society. Therefore Kṛṣṇa Himself appeared as Śrī Caitanya Mahāprabhu and ordered all Indians to take up the cause of distributing the knowledge of *Bhagavad-gītā* throughout the entire world:

yāre dekha, tāre kaha 'kṛṣṇa'—upadeśa
āmāra ājñāya guru hañā tāra' ei deśa

> Whomever you meet, instruct him on the teachings of Kṛṣṇa. In this way, on My order, become a spiritual master and deliver the people of this country. (*Caitanya-caritāṛmta* 2.7.128)

Although India has the sublime knowledge of *Bhagavad-gītā,* Indians have not done their proper duty of distributing it. Now, therefore, the Kṛṣṇa consciousness movement has been set up to distribute this knowledge as it is, without distortion. Although previously there were attempts to distribute the knowledge of *Bhagavad-gītā,* these attempts involved distortion and compromise with mundane knowledge. But now the Kṛṣṇa consciousness movement, without mundane compromises, is distributing *Bhagavad-gītā* as it is, and people are deriving the benefits of awakening to Kṛṣṇa consciousness and becoming devotees of Lord Kṛṣṇa. Therefore the proper distribution of knowledge has begun by which not only will the whole world benefit, but India's glory will be magnified in human society.... The real knowledge of *Bhagavad-gītā* was being choked by unscrupulous Indian leaders, with the result that India's culture, and knowledge of the Supreme, were being lost. Now, however, because Kṛṣṇa consciousness is spreading, the proper use of *Bhagavad-gītā* is being attempted.[68]

The Duty of Indians

Why Are You Neglecting Kṛṣṇa Consciousness?

Our request is: take to this Kṛṣṇa consciousness. If the foreigners can take to it very seriously, why not the Indians? It is Indians' knowledge. *Bhagavad-gītā* was spoken in India. Why are you neglecting it? Why you are not taking advantage?[69]

Remain as Indians, with Indian culture.[70]

Comment: "Be Indian, but live king-size like the Americans" is the idea of many modern Indian youths. But for all the bravado and phantasmagoria of "living king-size," everyone has to die ant-size, be punished in hell, and then be given a new body—dog-size or cat-size. Better to live sensibly, be thoughtful, and follow the Indian culture meant for spiritual elevation than to make a big foolish show of being a great sense enjoyer and end up becoming a dog.

Indians Should Preach Kṛṣṇa Consciousness

You have to make your life successful by reading *Bhagavad-gītā* and preaching the truth all over the world. Then the world will be happy and you will be happy. This is required.[71]

Those who are following in the footsteps of Śrī Caitanya Mahāprabhu should take the Lord's mission most seriously. In this Age of Kali, people are gradually becoming less than animals. Nevertheless, although they are eating the flesh of cows and are envious of brahminical culture, Śrī Caitanya Mahāprabhu is considering how to deliver them from this horrible condition of life. Thus He asks all Indians to take up His mission:

> *bhārata-bhūmite haila manuṣya-janma yāra*
> *janma sārthaka kari' kara para-upakāra*
>
> One who has taken his birth as a human being in the land of India (Bhārata-varṣa) should make his life successful and work for the benefit of all other people. (*Caitanya-caritāṛmta* 1.9.41)

It is therefore the duty of every advanced and cultured Indian to take this cause very seriously. All Indians should help the Kṛṣṇa consciousness movement in its progress, to the best of their ability. Then they will be considered real followers of Śrī Caitanya Mahāprabhu.[72]

One who has taken birth in the land of Bhārata-bhūmi, India, should take full advantage of his birth. He should become completely well versed in the knowledge of the Vedas and spiritual culture and should distribute the experience of Kṛṣṇa consciousness all over the world. People all over the world are madly engaging in sense gratification and in this way spoiling their human lives, with the risk that in the next life they may become animals or less. Human society should be saved from such a risky civilization and the danger of animalism by awakening to God consciousness, Kṛṣṇa consciousness. The Kṛṣṇa consciousness movement has been started for this purpose. Therefore unbiased men of the highest echelon should study the principles of the Kṛṣṇa consciousness movement and fully cooperate with this movement to save human society.[73]

Westerners Look to India for Enlightenment

Many people in America and Europe, especially the younger generation, are hankering after spiritual enlightenment. And they expect something from India. In a book recommended for study in New York University, a greatly learned scholar has written: "If you want to study religion as it is, then you have to go to India." So our Indian spiritual culture is still adored and worshipped by the learned section of every part of the world. And especially in America, Germany, and England, they are hankering after it. This transcendental knowledge, as distributed by Lord Caitanya, should be seriously taken up by the responsible Indians.[74]

Unite All Under One Flag

Indians have got a special prerogative for spreading this Kṛṣṇa consciousness movement all over the world. So why are you neglecting your duty? Prepare hundreds and thousands of preachers from India and send them outside. This rascaldom of always fighting with one another will be forgotten. All will be one under the flag of Kṛṣṇa consciousness. There is a need of such preachers. We should open a regular school or teaching institution for preparing preachers to send all over the world.[75]

Formerly India, Pakistan, Burma [Myanmar], and Ceylon [Śrī Lanka] were one. There is the chance of uniting all these different parts of India by Kṛṣṇa consciousness. You have to organize.[76]

The Best Welfare Activity

This *paropakāra,* welfare activities to spread Kṛṣṇa consciousness all over the world, is the most important business at the present moment. It will unite everyone politically, socially, culturally, religiously—in every way. Kṛṣṇa is the centre. That's a fact. It is making progress. And if we endeavour more and more, it will make more and more progress.[77]

The practical effect of our spreading the Kṛṣṇa consciousness movement all over the world is that now the most degraded debauchees are becoming the most elevated saints. This is only one Indian's humble service to the world. If all Indians had taken to this path, as advised by Lord Caitanya Mahāprabhu, India would have given a unique gift to the world, and thus India would have been glorified. Now, however, India is known as a poverty-stricken country, and whenever anyone from America or another opulent country goes to India, he sees many people lying by the footpaths for whom there are not even provisions for two meals a day. There are also institutions collecting money from all parts of the world in the name of welfare activities for poverty-stricken people, but they are spending it for their own sense gratification. Now, on the order of Śrī Caitanya Mahāprabhu, the Kṛṣṇa consciousness movement has been started, and people are benefiting from this movement. Therefore it is now the duty of the leading men of India to consider the importance of this movement and train many Indians to go outside of India to preach this cult. People will accept it, there will be cooperation among the Indian people and among the other people of the world, and the mission of Śrī Caitanya Mahāprabhu will then be fulfilled. Śrī Caitanya Mahāprabhu will then be glorified all over the world, and people will naturally be happy, peaceful, and prosperous, not only in this life but also in the next, for as stated in *Bhagavad-gītā,* anyone who understands Kṛṣṇa, the Supreme Personality of Godhead, will very easily get salvation, or freedom from the repetition of birth and death, and go back home, back to Godhead.

Śrī Caitanya Mahāprabhu therefore requests every Indian to become a preacher of His cult to save the world from disastrous confusion.

This is not only the duty of Indians but the duty of everyone, and we are very happy that American and European boys and girls are seriously cooperating with this movement. One should know definitely that the best welfare activity for all of human society is to awaken man's God consciousness, or Kṛṣṇa consciousness. Therefore everyone should help this great movement.[78]

Everyone born in India, especially as a human being, can achieve the supreme success through the Vedic literature and its practical application in life. When one is perfect, he can render service for the self-realization of the entire human society. This is the best way to perform humanitarian work.[79]

Of all welfare activities, this *kṛṣṇa-upadeśa*, instructing people about the primary principles of *Bhagavad-gītā*, is the best (*paropakāra*). People do not know how to become happy. They are simply struggling for existence by mental concoction. But there is no solution. Therefore every Indian should study *Bhagavad-gītā*, and if possible *Śrīmad-Bhāgavatam*, assimilate it, and preach all over the world. This is the duty of India. India has no other duty than *paropakāra* [spiritual welfare activities].[80]

[For more on why preaching Kṛṣṇa consciousness is the highest welfare activity—better than opening hospitals

or schools or feeding the poor—see chapter three of Preaching Is the Essence, *by Śrīla Prabhupāda.]*

Learn from the Kṛṣṇa Consciousness Movement

The difficulty with the Indians is that they are under the impression that they know everything and have not got to learn anything from us, but factually most of them have lost their original culture and have to learn so many things from this Kṛṣṇa consciousness movement.[81]

Indians Should Join This Movement

This Kṛṣṇa consciousness movement is an Indian movement. It is our movement. Kṛṣṇa came in India, and because India is such a glorified place, *puṇya-bhūmi*, even the demigods desire to take birth here. So it is not an ordinary land. Now every Indian should take part in this great movement—every Indian. That is Caitanya Mahāprabhu's order.[82]

Indians Should Become Gurus and Save the World

If you simply do this missionary work and say, "Kṛṣṇa is the Supreme," then you become a great devotee. You become a guru. Why do people not do so? It is not a very difficult task. This is Caitanya

Mahāprabhu's mission. He said, "By My order you become a guru." Indians especially are advised to become gurus because Indians, however fallen they may be, still have respect for Kṛṣṇa. In every home they perform Kṛṣṇa's Janmāṣṭamī. Therefore Indians are fortunate. They recognize Kṛṣṇa. Now, to become a little more advanced, let them act as Kṛṣṇa's servant.[83]

Everyone is advised to become a guru—especially those born in India. They can easily take to the Kṛṣṇa consciousness movement because in their blood there is Kṛṣṇa consciousness, on account of taking birth in this holy land of Bhārata-varṣa. So every Indian is expected to take to this Kṛṣṇa consciousness movement and spread it outside India. There are many people who are hankering after it.[84]

Caitanya Mahāprabhu instructed everyone to become a guru. The world is suffering for want of Kṛṣṇa consciousness. That was His mission. He wanted everyone from India to become a guru and preach outside: "Become a guru on My order, and deliver your country or other countries."

"But I have no qualification, no education. How I can become guru?"

Caitanya Mahāprabhu says, *āmāra ājñāya:* "By My order."

"Then what is Your order, Sir?"

"My order is *yāre dekha tāre kaha 'kṛṣṇa'-upadeśa.* This is My order. Simply explain what Kṛṣṇa has said, or what has been said about Kṛṣṇa."

That is *kṛṣṇa-upadeśa.* Simply preach *kṛṣṇa-upadeśa,* then you become a guru. Not only that, He has empowered all Indians:

bhārata-bhūmite haila manuṣya-janma yāra
janma sārthaka kari' kara para-upakāra.

To spread this Kṛṣṇa consciousness movement is the best welfare activity in human society.[85]

Be Careful

We shall be careful, at least in India, that we may not glide down more and more to the animal platform of life.[86]

Looking to the Future

Comment: Modern India has so many problems that one may think religion to be just one more of them. "Let us first feed people and solve all other problems," we hear people say, "then we can think about religion." Unfortunately, however much we try, we will never be able to solve all problems in this material world, for its very nature is to be full of problems.

However, if the people of India take up the chanting of Hare Kṛṣṇa and seriously cooperate with the Kṛṣṇa consciousness movement, then by the grace of God they will see myriad problems disappear as if they never existed. India can again be a happy, civilized nation, a model for all others on earth, if she revives her tradition of God consciousness. How this can happen may be inexplicable by material understanding, but it is certainly possible by the blessings of God.

Indian Culture Can Be Revived

There is no hopelessness. If we revive Kṛṣṇa consciousness in a systematic way, within a very short time we can revive our original Indian culture on the basis of the teachings of Lord Kṛṣṇa and the *Bhagavad-gītā*. So we have to work very hard for this purpose, and if you follow the path of Śrī Caitanya Mahāprabhu it will be very easily done.[87]

There is all-round guidance in *Bhagavad-gītā* for all matters—social, political, religious, educational, cultural, and philosophical. But instead of taking guidance from *Bhagavad-gītā*, they are now enamoured by the external feature of modern civilization. *Na te viduḥ svārtha-gatiṁ hi viṣṇum:* "They do not know that the supreme self-interest is to know Viṣṇu." (*Bhāgavatam* 7.5.31) Still there is time before complete ruination, if we take this Kṛṣṇa consciousness movement seriously.[88]

The Kṛṣṇa Consciousness Movement Is the Only Hope

We have given up our own culture and are imitating the foreigners. That also we cannot do very properly because in India we are meant for a different purpose. These rascals have forgotten their own culture. They have accepted so many *anarthas* (unwanted things). Take, for example, drinking wine. Is it a very necessary thing? Drinking tea, is it necessary? Smoking bidis? These are all foolishness. The society is unnecessarily creating entanglement, *anartha*. This Kṛṣṇa consciousness is the only remedy for curbing this unnecessary so-called civilization.[89]

The presidents and chief executives in the Age of Kali are simply tax collectors who do not care whether religious principles are observed. Indeed, the chief executives of the present day introduce all kinds of sinful activity, especially illicit sex, intoxication, animal killing, and gambling. These sinful activities are now very prominently manifested in India. Although a hundred years ago these four principles of sinful life were strictly prohibited in the families of India, they have now been introduced into every Indian family; therefore they cannot follow religious principles. In contrast to the principles of the kings of old, the modern state is concerned only with propaganda for levying taxes and is no longer responsible for the spiritual welfare of the citizens. The state is now callous to religious principles. *Śrīmad-Bhāgavatam* predicts that in Kali-yuga the government will be entrusted with *dasyu-dharma,* which means the occupational duty of rogues and thieves. Modern heads of state are rogues and thieves who plunder the citizens instead of giving them protection. Rogues and thieves plunder without regard for law, but in this Age of Kali, as stated in *Śrīmad-Bhāgavatam,* the lawmakers themselves plunder the citizens. The next prediction to be fulfilled, which is already coming to pass, is that because of the sinful activities of the citizens and the government, rain will become increasingly scarce. Gradually there will be complete drought and no production of food grains. People will be reduced to eating flesh and seeds, and many good, spiritually inclined people will have to forsake their homes because they will be too harassed by drought, taxation, and famine. The Kṛṣṇa consciousness movement is the only hope to save the world from such devastation. It is the most scientific and authorized movement for the actual welfare of the whole human society.[90]

India is now in a miserable condition by its poverty and natural atrocities like floods, earthquakes, etc. Your suggestion that this can only be solved by Lord Kṛṣṇa, the omnipotent, is also right. Therefore if you want to do something for India, the only remedial measure that you can take is to spread Kṛṣṇa consciousness. You say that materialism is trying to dominate, but at the same time religious faith is also progressing. Two things cannot go on simultaneously. Actually India is the country of religion. The present government policy to kill the religious faith of the people is resulting in frustration of religious life because it is not organizedly taught. But by nature the people of India have a hankering for spiritual advancement, and therefore the present situation is a natural result of the clash between two opposite ideals. In this case also, the best treatment is to give the people scientific religious ideas, which are very clearly stated in the *Bhagavad-gītā*. But unfortunately, unscrupulous and rascal so-called scholars, religionists, and philosophers have misinterpreted the teachings of Lord Kṛṣṇa in the *Bhagavad-gītā* and have misled the whole population. *Bhagavad-gītā* is popular not only in India, but also all over the world. Unfortunately, the real idea has been distorted. We have therefore presented our *Bhagavad-gītā As It Is*. I have tried to explain in this book the real purpose of the *Bhagavad-gītā*. *Bhagavad-gītā* is the authorized book to teach people how to love Kṛṣṇa, the Supreme Personality of Godhead. There is nothing else except devotional service to the Lord described there, but great politicians have misinterpreted the sunshine-like clear statements of *Bhagavad-gītā* with a cloud of mental concoctions. So if you think seriously to improve the condition of India, you can begin even on a small scale the propagation of Kṛṣṇa consciousness, and if you do it seriously and sincerely, surely you will be successful.[91]

Overcoming the Demonic Culture

Actually there is no civilization at the present moment. They are simply cats and dogs and fighting one another. This is not civilization. Atheists and demons are predominating. Because they have got big, big skyscraper buildings and many motorcars, India has become victimized: "Oh, without motorcars and skyscraper buildings we are condemned." So they are trying to imitate. They have forgotten their own culture, the best culture, the Vedic culture. So for the first time we are trying to conquer over the demoniac culture with the Vedic culture. If you want to make the human society happy, give them this culture of Kṛṣṇa consciousness. If you become involved in this demoniac culture, then the *saṁsāra-cakra,* the wheel of repetition of birth and death, will go on. You cannot stop it. It is not possible. But if you take to Kṛṣṇa consciousness, then it is possible.[92]

The Peace Formula

With one man's endeavour, my teeny effort, so many outsiders have become attracted to Kṛṣṇa consciousness. Unless there is something substantial, why will they be attracted? They are not illiterate. They are not fools. They are not poor. Why are they attracted? Because there is something to be learned from Kṛṣṇa consciousness. So if this Kṛṣṇa consciousness movement is systematically spread all over the world, the face of the world will change. That's a fact. *Sarve sukhino bhavantu:* "Let everyone become happy." This is the Vedic mission. And how can they be happy? Not by mental concoction. That is not possible. Human society cannot be happy without Kṛṣṇa consciousness. Kṛṣṇa says in *Bhagavad-gītā* (5.29):

bhoktāraṁ yajña-tapasāṁ
sarva-loka-maheśvaram
suhṛdaṁ sarva-bhūtānāṁ
jñātvā māṁ śāntim ṛcchati

> A person in full consciousness of Me, knowing Me to be the ultimate beneficiary of all sacrifices and austerities, the Supreme Lord of all planets and demigods, and the benefactor and well-wisher of all living entities, attains peace from the pangs of material miseries.

If you want *śānti*, individually or collectively, nationally or internationally, then you must become Kṛṣṇa conscious.[93]

India Will Be Glorified

This Hare Kṛṣṇa movement is Indian culture. If the leaders of Indian culture take it seriously, certainly India's glories will be magnified. In foreign countries India is much advertised as a poverty-stricken country. But if India can give her spiritual culture, Kṛṣṇa consciousness, she will be glorified everywhere.[94]

The difficulty is that India is nowhere. They are trying to imitate Western life, but from a materialistic or technical point of view, they are one hundred years back. There is one thing I am experiencing: if India's spiritual asset is distributed, that will increase India's honour. Because everywhere I go, people still adore Indian culture. If this treasure house of India's spiritual knowledge is properly distributed, at least people outside of India will understand that they are getting something from India.[95]

Everything is in *Bhagavad-gītā*, all solutions—social, political, and economical. It is our property. It was spoken in India, and it was desired that all Indians should learn it and spread the knowledge all over the world, on Caitanya Mahāprabhu's order. But the rascals are doing nothing. Other parts of the world are in darkness. There is a great necessity of spreading the knowledge of *Bhagavad-gītā* all over the world. The customers are ready. So if you want the glory of India, if you want to glorify your life, just study *Bhagavad-gītā As It Is* and spread it all over the world. You'll be honoured. Single-handed, whatever I have done, they are thinking it is wonderful. And if we get many, many people to go outside India and preach this gospel of *Bhagavad-gītā,* they will be benefited and you will be glorified. Your country will be glorified. Spread this message of *Bhagavad-gītā*. It is a fact; it is not a story. People are fed up with this wrong type of civilization.[96]

India Can Save, Uplift, and Lead the World

The real success or fulfilment of the mission of human life can be achieved in India, Bhārata-varṣa, because in Bhārata-varṣa the purpose of life and the method for achieving success are evident. People should take advantage of the opportunity afforded by Bhārata-varṣa, and this is especially so for those who are following the principles of *varṇāśrama-dharma.* If we do not take to the principles of *varṇāśrama-dharma* by accepting the four social orders (*brāhmaṇa, kṣatriya, vaiśya,* and *śūdra*) and the four orders of spiritual life (*brahmacārī, gṛhastha, vānaprastha,* and *sannyāsī*), there can be no question of success in life. Unfortunately, because of the influence of Kali-yuga, everything is now being lost. The inhabitants of Bhārata-varṣa are gradually becoming degraded *mlecchas* and *yavanas.* How then will they teach others? Therefore, this Kṛṣṇa consciousness movement has been started not only for the inhabitants of Bhārata-varṣa but for all the people of the world, as announced by Śrī Caitanya Mahāprabhu. There is still time, and if the inhabitants of Bhārata-varṣa take this movement of Kṛṣṇa consciousness seriously, the entire world will be saved from gliding down to a hellish condition.[97]

I wish to appeal to all the leading men of India to accept this movement very seriously and give us all facility to spread this movement throughout the world. Then there will be a very happy condition, not only in India but all over the world.[98]

People are hankering after this Kṛṣṇa culture. Prepare yourself to present *Bhagavad-gītā* as it is. Then India will conquer all over the world by Kṛṣṇa culture.[99]

Saving India

At least in India sinful activities should be stopped. That is my ambition. India cannot go in that way. We have got so much stock of knowledge. Other rascals may be misled, but in India at least there must be an ideal class. That I want. Why should India's name be defamed? They are following in the same blind man's way. Therefore I repeatedly invite you all to come, join, and understand.[100]

Kṛṣṇa Conscious Government

We are requesting everywhere, not only in India, but all over the world, to act according to the order of the Supreme Personality of Godhead. Gradually they are accepting the principle. So why not in India? The *Bhagavad-gītā* was spoken in India. Still in India there are many devotees, many Kṛṣṇa conscious persons. I wish that the government may be conducted under the guidance of Lord Kṛṣṇa. The codes and orders, the rules and regulations, are all stated in *Bhagavad-gītā*. Consciously or unconsciously, we accept *Bhagavad-gītā*. That is our Indian culture, Vedic culture.[101]

Youth of India

Youth as Victims

It is understood that one who has taken birth in India tried to cultivate spiritual culture in his previous birth. Therefore he has been given the opportunity to take birth in India. India is so fortunate. But as soon as he takes birth, the rascal leaders spoil him—the rascal father spoils him, the rascal teacher spoils him. So what can they do, the poor younger generation? They are being taught "Spiritual culture is useless. Because we are so spiritually inclined, the foreigners came and lorded over us. Now give up all this nonsense. Become a technologist." This is going on. This will not make us happy.[102]

Although India is the land of spiritual culture, our children have no connection with *Bhagavad-gītā* in the schools and colleges. They are simply trained up for sense gratification. Sense gratification is meant to be suppressed, but they are being given education in it. They do not know what is *karma* (proper action) and what is *vikarma* (improper action). When the students become disobedient, create riots, and burn buses, then the older generation lament. But why you have educated the students like that? Who is responsible for this? The rascals do not know.[103]

They are thinking, "I have become civilized. I have become educated. Therefore I shall not practice religion." So are the Western Kṛṣṇa devotees not educated? Are they not civilized? Why are Indian boys refusing? That is my question. They are losing the opportunity of taking birth in India. They are so fortunate to take their birth in India, but they are refusing this culture. That is the effect of modern education.[104]

Young People Should Join This Movement

We invite educated, intellectual young men to come forward to study this movement very seriously and help spread it all over India.[105]

The younger generation of India should come forward, join this movement, and spread Kṛṣṇa consciousness all over the world.[106]

You [young boys] should be very responsible. Caitanya Mahāprabhu specifically said, *bhārata-bhūmite haila manuṣya-janma yāra/* (Anyone who has taken birth as a human being in the land of Bhārata-varṣa) *janma sārthaka kari' kara para-upakāra* (just make your life successful and do welfare activities for others). So you must realize—because in India you have got this Kṛṣṇa science, or spiritual culture, left by so many sages and saintly persons. You cannot make your life successful or glorious simply by imitating the West. You cannot compete with them. Realize your own assets and distribute to the world. That will make you glorious.[107]

East and West Should Cooperate

Comment: Śrīla Prabhupāda once said, "As did Lord Rāma, I crossed the ocean to the land of the asuras *and brought back Lakṣmī to India." (Rāma brought Lakṣmī as Sītā; Prabhupāda brought Lakṣmī as money for building temples.) He also likened India to Sarasvatī (spiritual knowledge) and the West to Lakṣmī (material prosperity), and proposed that Sarasvatī and Lakṣmī combine for the upliftment of mankind.*

Every human being born in India should take up this cult of Śrī Caitanya Mahāprabhu. They can take it, because it is their birthright—because this *Bhāgavatam* is produced in India and *Bhagavad-gītā* is produced in India. That is the glory of India. So the sons of India, those who are Indians, those who are proud of becoming Indian, should take up this mission. *Janma sārthaka kari:* first of all make your life successful by understanding *Bhagavad-gītā* and *Śrīmad-Bhāgavatam.* Understand *Śrīmad-Bhāgavatam* and *Bhagavad-gītā,* and preach this knowledge all over the world.

Such knowledge is wanting all over the world. The Western countries might have advanced in technical knowledge, but they have no knowledge about the science of God. That is lacking. So East and West should cooperate. You have got some knowledge—I take advantage of it. I have got some knowledge—you take advantage of it. This is cooperation. Now, people all over the world are trying to imitate the Western type of civilization. That is not bad. Do it. But you also do something so that Westerners may also take your knowledge. That is cooperation. Why are you silent on this point? Therefore, because Indians and the Indian government have failed to do this duty, India is known as a beggar country all over the world.[108]

The Lame Man and the Blind Man

The tract of land south of the Himalayan Mountains is the land of India, which was known as Bhārata-varṣa. When a living entity takes birth in Bhārata-varṣa he is considered to be most fortunate. Indeed, Caitanya Mahāprabhu has stated:

bhārata-bhūmite haila manuṣya-janma yāra
janma sārthaka kari' kara para-upakāra

(*Caitanya-caritāmṛta 1.9.41*)

Thus whoever takes birth in the land of Bhārata-varṣa attains all the facilities of life. He may take advantage of all these facilities for both material and spiritual advancement and thus make his life successful. After attaining the goal of life, one may distribute his knowledge and experience all over the world for humanitarian purposes. In other words, one who takes birth in the land of Bhārata-varṣa by virtue of his past pious activities gets full facility to develop the human form of life. In India, the climatic condition is such that one can live very peacefully without being disturbed by material conditions. Indeed, during the time of Mahārāja Yudhiṣṭhira or Lord Rāmacandra, people were free from all anxieties. There was not even extreme cold or extreme heat. The three kinds of miserable conditions—*ādhyātmika*, *ādhibhautika*, and *ādhidaivika* (miseries inflicted by the body and mind itself, those inflicted by other living entities, and natural disturbances)—were all absent during the reign of Lord Rāmacandra or Mahārāja Yudhiṣṭhira. But at present, compared to other countries on earth, India is artificially disturbed. Despite these material disturbances, however, the country's culture is such that one can easily attain the goal of life, namely salvation, or liberation from material bondage. Thus in order to take birth in India one must have performed many pious activities in a past life.

In this verse the word *lakṣita-lakṣaṇām* indicates that the human body attained in Bhārata-varṣa is very auspicious. Vedic culture is full of knowledge, and a person born in India can fully take advantage of Vedic cultural knowledge and the cultural system known as *varṇāśrama-dharma*. Even at the present time, as we travel all over the world, we see that in some countries human beings have many material facilities but no facilities for spiritual advancement. We find everywhere the defects of one-sided facilities and a lack of full facilities. A blind man can walk but not see, and a lame man cannot walk but can see. *Andha-*

paṅgu-nyāya: the blind man may take the lame man over his shoulder, and as he walks, the lame man may give him directions. Thus combined they may work, but individually neither the blind man nor the lame man can walk successfully. Similarly, this human form of life is meant for the advancement of spiritual life and for keeping the material necessities in order. Especially in the Western countries there are ample facilities for material comforts, but no one has any idea of spiritual advancement. Many are hankering after spiritual advancement, but many cheaters come, take advantage of their money, bluff them, and go away. Fortunately the Kṛṣṇa consciousness movement is there to give all facilities for both material and spiritual advancement. In this way, people in the Western countries may take advantage of this movement. In India any man in the villages, unaffected by the industrial cities of India, can still live in any condition and make spiritual advancement. The body has been called the city of nine gates, and these nine gates include two eyes, two ears, two nostrils, one mouth, genitals, and a rectum. When the nine gates are clean and working properly, it is to be understood that the body is healthy. In India these nine gates are kept clean by the villagers who rise early in the morning, bathe in the well or rivers, go to the temples to attend *maṅgala-ārati,* chant the Hare Kṛṣṇa *mahā-mantra,* and take *prasāda.* In this way one can take advantage of all the facilities of human life. We are gradually introducing this system in different centres in our Society in the Western countries. One who takes advantage of it becomes more and more enlightened in spiritual life. At the present moment, India may be compared to the lame man, and the Western countries to the blind man. For the past two thousand years India has been subjugated by the rule of foreigners, and the legs of progress have been broken. In the Western countries the eyes of the people have become blind due to the dazzling glitter of material opulence. The blind man of the Western countries and the lame man of India should combine together in this Kṛṣṇa consciousness movement. Then the lame man of India can walk with the help of the Westerner, and the blind Westerner can see with the help of the lame man. In short, the material advancement of the Western countries and the spiritual assets of India should combine for the elevation of all human society.[109]

The West Must Look to India

In no country other than India have the great sages endeavoured so much for the realization of the spirit self. It is admitted that in the Western countries the people have done their best to advance in the culture of material science, centred on the material body and mind. But it is admitted, also, that notwithstanding all such advancement of material knowledge in the West, the people in general are suffering the pangs of the poisonous effects of materialism because they have cared very little for the culture of spiritual science.

Great thinkers in the Western countries must therefore look to the people of India if the message of Godhead, of genuine spiritualism, is to reach their ears.[110]

Unite and Change the World

The *Padma Purāṇa* states that there are 8,400,000 different species of life, of which 400,000 are human. Out of them, one who is born in India is a first-class human being. That is a fact. Unfortunately, we are missing the chance. Therefore Caitanya Mahāprabhu says, *bhārata-bhūmite haila manuṣya-janma yāra*. Indians should know that after performing many pious activities, one gets birth in India (*bhārata-bhūmite*). So try to understand Kṛṣṇa. There is facility. There are *śāstras*. Kṛṣṇa personally speaks *Bhagavad-gītā*. Vyāsadeva speaks about Kṛṣṇa in the *Śrīmad-Bhāgavatam*. We are neglecting. We have become such rascals and fools. This is not India's business, to imitate economic development: "Money, money, money, money, money." India's business is to understand Kṛṣṇa. *Athāto brahma-jijñāsā:* "human life is meant for enquiry into the absolute truth." These Americans and Europeans have not come here to see how much you are economically and industrially developed. They have got enough of this—more than enough. They don't care for it. The modern young men are fed up. They have come here to understand Kṛṣṇa. Therefore we are constructing this centre. Let everyone come, from all over the world. It is India's business to understand Kṛṣṇa and help them. The Kṛṣṇa consciousness movement is a very serious movement. On this platform, the whole world can be united. It is not an ordinary movement. Try to understand Kṛṣṇa.[111]

I have given them the philosophy of "American money and Indian culture." Combined together, the face of the world will change. Don't keep Indian culture airtight, and don't keep American money for sense gratification. Use it for Kṛṣṇa.[112]

Make the Whole World Hindustan

Interviewer: Why did you choose to go to America and propagate the teachings of Lord Kṛṣṇa in a Western country?

Prabhupāda: Because Indian people, being subjugated for at least one thousand years, have lost their original culture. Being poverty-stricken, they are simply after money, by hook or crook. In the *Bhagavad-gītā* it is said, *bhogaiśvarya-prasaktānāṁ tayāpahṛta-cetasām*: "persons who have lost their consciousness because of too much attachment to material enjoyment cannot understand Kṛṣṇa consciousness."

Interviewer: Oriental philosophies in general, and Kṛṣṇa consciousness in particular, have found a lot of devotees in the Western civilization. What is the main reason for this?

Prabhupāda: You are thinking this is Oriental civilization, but that is not the fact. The fact is this is human civilization. There is no question of East and West.

Interviewer: Do you feel that your success in the West is an indication of the need being felt by the Western man that has been lacking in spiritual ideologies?

Prabhupāda: Yes. The Westerners are very intelligent and materially advanced. But spiritually they are not. Therefore they are coming to me, a poor Indian. Not only me—any swami who goes, they crowd to him. Unfortunately, the other swamis go to exploit and cheat them. Neither do they know what is spiritual life, nor could they give it to them. For the last two hundred years or so the swamis have been going, but not a single person became a Kṛṣṇa devotee in the history of the Western world. But now we are giving *Bhagavad-gītā As It Is,* and hundreds and thousands are coming.

Interviewer: Swamiji, it's been sometimes said that India has too much philosophy and the West has too much materialism. Where is the right balance in this modern world?

Prabhupāda: The balance is that there should be a reciprocal exchange of gifts. What you haven't got, I give you; what I haven't got, you give me. Then the world will be united. But our India followed the principle of begging: "Give me men. Give me money. Give me wheat. Give me rice. Give me war materials."

Simply begging. So we must give something. This is the first time we are giving something. Otherwise, India was simply a beggar to the Western countries. For their technical education they are going to the Western countries, and when there is war, they are asking America, "Please give us war materials." And when they give war materials to Pakistan we become envious. We are lamenting because we have lost a portion of the country as Pakistan and are fighting since then. This was a plan by the British government to divide them in such a way they will perpetually fight, they will never be happy. But if you take this Kṛṣṇa consciousness movement very seriously, you can make the whole world Hindustan.[113]

Hindus and Muslims

How the Muslim Population Increased

To convert a Hindu into a Muslim was an easy affair in those days. If a Muslim simply sprinkled water on the body of a Hindu, it was supposed that the Hindu had already become a Muslim. During the transition of the British in Bangladesh during the last Hindu-Muslim riots, many Hindus were converted into Muslims by having cow's flesh forcibly pushed into their mouth. Hindu society was so rigid at the time of Lord Caitanya that if a Hindu were converted into a Muslim, there was no chance of his being reformed. In this way the Muslim population in India increased. None of the Muslims came from outside; social customs somehow or other forced Hindus to become Muslims, with no chance of returning to Hindu society. Emperor Aurangzeb also inaugurated a tax that Hindus had to pay because of their being Hindus. Thus all the poor Hindus of the lower class voluntarily became Muslims to avoid the tax. In this way the Muslim population in India increased.[114]

More than five hundred years ago in India, the Hindus were so rigid and strict that if a Muslim would sprinkle a little water from his pitcher upon a Hindu, the Hindu would be immediately ostracized. Recently, in 1947, during the partition days, there was a big riot between Hindus and Muslims, especially in Bengal. The Hindus were forcibly made to eat cow's flesh, and consequently they began crying, thinking that they had become Muslims. Actually the Muslims in India did not come from the country of the Muslims, but Hindus instituted the custom that somehow or other if one contacted a Muslim, he became a Muslim. Rūpa and Sanātana Gosvāmī were born in a high *brāhmaṇa* family, but because they accepted employment under a Muslim government they were considered Muslims. Subuddhi Rāya was sprinkled with water from the pitcher of a Muslim, and consequently he was condemned to become a Muslim. Later, Aurangzeb, the Muslim emperor, introduced a tax especially meant for Hindus. Being oppressed in the Hindu community, many low-caste Hindus preferred to become Muslims. In this way the Muslim population increased.[115]

Hindus and Muslims Lived Peacefully

Hindus and Muslims used to live together peacefully. It is not a fact that Muslims were always aggressive. Otherwise, how they could rule over India for eight hundred years?[116]

In India, even in the interior villages, all the Hindu and Muslim communities used to live very peacefully by establishing a relationship between them. The young men called the elderly members of the village by the name *cācā* or *kākā*, uncle, and men of the same age called each other *dādā*, brother. The relationship was very friendly. There were even invitations from Muslim houses to Hindu houses and from Hindu houses to Muslim houses. Both the Hindus and the Muslims accepted the invitations to go to each others' houses to attend ceremonial functions. Even until fifty or sixty years ago, the relationship between Hindus and Muslims was very friendly and there were no disturbances. We do not find any Hindu-Muslim riots in the history of India, even during the days of the Muslims' rule over the country. Conflict between Hindus and Muslims was created by polluted politicians, especially foreign rulers, and thus the situation gradually became so degraded that India was divided into Hindustan and Pakistan. Fortunately, the remedy to unite not only the Hindus and Muslims but all communities and all nations can still be implemented by the Hare Kṛṣṇa movement on the strong basic platform of love of Godhead.[117]

We actually saw during the partition days in India that although Hindus and Muslims were living together peacefully, manipulation by politicians suddenly aroused feelings of hatred between them, and thus the Hindus and Muslims killed one another over politics.[118]

"Religious" Fighting Is Foolishness

In Hindu-Muslim riots, Hindus break mosques and Muslims break idols in Hindu temples. They think,

"We have finished the Hindus' God." The Hindus also think, "We have broken their mosque. Therefore we have broken their God." This is foolishness. They are not *jñānīs* [men of knowledge]. Those with a real conception of God have no quarrel with each other.[119]

According to Vedic authorities, the first-class religious system is tested thus: *sa vai puṁsāṁ paro dharmo yato bhaktir adhokṣaje* [unmotivated, uninterrupted devotional service to the Supreme Personality of Godhead]. Everyone is eager to fight on behalf of his own religion. The Christians, Buddhists, Muslims, and Hindus all maintain their religions to be best. Throughout history, fights have been waged between religions. During the Crusades the Christians fought the Muslims, and in India there are often fights between the Hindus and the Muslims. What is the meaning of such fights? If one is actually God conscious he knows God, so what is the possibility of his fighting? If a person is actually a devotee of God he can see that God is one. God cannot possibly be two, nor can the Hindus have one God and the Christians or Muslims another.[120]

The *Īśopaniṣad* teaches, *īśāvāsyam idaṁ sarvaṁ:* "Nothing belongs to you. Everything belongs to God." It is said that God laughs when two parties fight for land. In the partition days, the Hindus and Muslims fought. When both of them died and lay strewn all over the street and were asked, "Now, whose land is it?" nobody replied. God's land will remain here. We simply fight: "This is my land." This is all illusion.[121]

Ten Points for Indira Gandhi

On 22 August 1975, Śrīla Prabhupāda had an appointment with Indira Gandhi. In a pocket notebook, he had listed ten points to present to her. But because on that day Mrs. Gandhi was disturbed by rumours of a threat to her life, Śrīla Prabhupāda did not raise his proposal. Nonetheless, these notes are testimony of Śrīla Prabhupāda's vision for a Kṛṣṇa conscious India. The ten points were:

(1) Grant immigration for 500 foreigners.

Comment: *Śrīla Prabhupāda wanted many Western devotees to come to India to learn the culture of Kṛṣṇa consciousness and also to preach.*

(2) All M.P.s initiated *brāhmaṇas.*

Comment: *This means initiated as Vaiṣṇava* brāhmaṇas, *following the regulations of Kṛṣṇa conscious life.*

(3) Sanjay the King, Indira Queen Mother.

Comment: *Śrīla Prabhupāda always stressed that monarchy is superior to democracy. The best system of government is that shown by pious rulers like Lord Rāma and Mahārāja Yudhiṣṭhira. A God conscious king should take guidance from ideal* brāhmaṇas *and rule the country for the sake of dharma. Śrīla Prabhupāda wanted to reestablish this system.*

(4) Close slaughterhouses.

(5) Chanting.

(6) Meat-eaters at home. No public meat-eating.

Comment: *Slaughterhouses and butcher shops should be closed. Then meat-eaters would have to personally kill any animal they wanted to eat. While meat-eating cannot be fully stopped, such restrictions would certainly reduce this ghastly practice.*

(7) Prostitution punishable.

(8) No religious group except *Bhagavad-gītā As It Is.*

(9) All government officers must join *kīrtana* at least twice a day.

Comment: *Among the people in general,* kīrtana *should be promoted, but for government officers it should be compulsory. Unless the leaders of society are ideal, the country must necessarily be spoiled. The regular chanting of Hare Kṛṣṇa will do much to cure the diseases of self-interest and corruption crippling India's administrative system.*

(10) Support Kṛṣṇa consciousness all over the world.

Comment: *If the Indian government were to vigorously and intelligently promote Kṛṣṇa consciousness nationally and internationally, a worldwide revolution of consciousness would take place, and soon India would be respected as the spiritual guide of all nations. The world is ready. Is India?*

Acknowledgements

Grateful thanks to Guru-Kṛṣṇa Dāsa, who edited this revised edition; to John Morgan, who offered valuable editorial suggestions; to Mādhava dāsa, who designed the cover; to Śrī Giridhārī Dāsa, who oversaw the printing; to Rādhā-rasika-rāja Dāsa and Indira Meshram, who proofread the manuscript; and to all others who helped in various ways.

Notes

Abbreviations

Cc: *Śrī Caitanya-caritāmṛta* (1: *Ādi-līlā*; 2: *Madhya-līlā*; 3: *Antya-līlā*)
MG: *Message of Godhead*
SB: *Śrīmad-Bhāgavatam* (1: First Canto; 2: Second Canto; and so on)
Numbers before references correspond to endnotes.

Caitanya Mahāprabhu's Mission

1 Cc 1.9.41.
2 Conversation, 10 Aug 76.
3 Conversation, 24 Jan 77.

The Glories of Bhārata-varṣa

4 Conversation, 22 Dec 76.
5 SB 7.14.29.
6 MG, ch.1.
7 MG, ch.2.
8 Cc 3.4.98.
9 SB 5.19.23.
10 SB 5.19.29.
11 Lecture, 30 Mar 74.
12 Lecture, 14 Apr 72.
13 Lecture, 31 Aug 72.
14 SB 4.21.12.
15 SB 3.1.20.
16 Lecture, 24 Oct 7.
17 Lecture, 6 Nov 70.
18 Lecture, 26 Oct 66.

India's Present Condition

19 Lecture, 20 Mar 75.
20 Lecture, 22 Dec 75.

21 Lecture, 18 Oct 75.
22 Letter to Pope Paul VI, 3 Aug 68.
23 Conversation, 31 Jan 77.
24 Conversation, 7 Jan 77.
25 Cc 3.9.142.
26 SB 7.14.29.
27 SB 10.5.8.
28 Lecture, 12 Dec 72.
29 Lecture, 3 Apr 74.
30 Lecture, 19 Dec 70.
31 Conversation, 21 Jan 77.

Causes of India's Downfall

32 SB 2.3.14.
33 Lecture, 14 Nov 74.
34 Lecture, 17 Aug 66.
35 Conversation, 27 Mar 74.
36 SB 1.19.4.
37 Lecture, 4 Apr 74.
38 Lecture, 13 Nov 73.
39 Lecture, 22 May 69.
40 Letter, 18 Sep 76.
41 Lecture, 12 Dec 72.
42 Lecture, 6 Mar 75.
43 Cc 2.1.197.
44 Lecture, 6 Nov 72.
45 Lecture, 3 Oct 73.
46 Lecture, 25 Oct 73.
47 Interview, 25 Mar 76.
48 Letter, 16 Mar 69.
49 Lecture, 30 Aug 75.
50 Conversation, 22 Aug 76.
51 Letter, 14 Nov 75.
52 Lecture, 13 Dec 72.
53 Letter, 26 Jan 76.
54 Conversation, 9 Jan 77.
55 Lecture, 22 Feb 74.
56 Conversation, 24 Apr 77.

57 Interview, 25 Mar 76.
58 Conversation, 5 Jul 76.
59 Conversation, 2 Jan 77.
60 Conversation, 16 Sep 76.
61 Lecture, 4 Nov 72.
62 Lecture, 12 Apr 73.
63 Lecture, 27 Oct 72.
64 Lecture, 6 Jun 74.
65 Lecture, 1 Mar 71.
66 Lecture, 18 Aug 71.
67 Lecture, 4 Sep 72.
68 SB 10.2.19.

The Duty of Indians

69 Lecture, 1 Jan 76.
70 Lecture, 20 Jun 76.
71 Lecture, 4 Apr 74.
72 Cc 3.3.51.
73 Cc 3.4.98
74 Lecture, 28 Jul 68.
75 Lecture, 7 Apr 71.
76 Conversation, 19 Apr 77.
77 Lecture, 29 Mar 71.
78 Cc 1.9.41.
79 SB 6.16.58.
80 Lecture, 7 Nov 74.
81 Letter, 27 May 70.
82 Conversation, 26 Dec 76.
83 Conversation, 3 Dec 76.
84 Lecture, 24 Nov 75.
85 Lecture, 7 Nov 74.
86 Lecture, 22 Jan 77.

Looking to the Future

87 Letter, 18 Sep 76.
88 Letter, 14 Nov 75.
89 Lecture, 15 Apr 76.
90 SB 5.2.1.

91 Letter, 8 Jul 69.
92 Lecture, 28 Feb 76.
93 Lecture, 7 Nov 74.
94 Letter, 1 Nov 76.
95 Conversation, 22 Jun 77.
96 Lecture, 24 Feb 74.
97 SB 5.19.10.
98 Letter, quoted in *Science of Self-realization* ch. 6.
99 Conversation, 31 Mar 71.
100 Conversation, 22 Mar 77.
101 Conversation, 22 Aug 76.

Youth of India

102 Lecture, 15 Apr 76.
103 Lecture, 5 Apr 74.
104 Lecture, 19 Dec 70.
105 Lecture, 20 Apr 75.
106 Lecture, 29 Mar 71.
107 Lecture, 19 Dec 70.

East and West Should Cooperate

108 Lecture, 23 Jul 73.
109 SB 4.25.13.
110 MG, ch. 2.
111 Lecture, 9 Aug 74.
112 Conversation, 13 Oct 77.
113 Interview, 25 Mar 75.

Hindus and Muslims

114 Cc 1.17.128.
115 Cc 2.25.193.
116 Lecture, 8 Apr 74.
117 Cc 1.17.148.
118 SB 6.2.5-6.
119 Lecture, 9 Oct 66.
120 Lecture, 5 Sep 72.
121 Lecture, 14 Apr 66.

Other Books by Bhakti Vikāsa Swami

A Beginner's Guide to Kṛṣṇa Consciousness

Read this book and improve your life!

All you need to know to get started in Kṛṣṇa consciousness. Easy-to-understand guidance on daily practices that bring us closer to Kṛṣṇa. Packed with practical information. Suitable both for devotees living in an ashram or at home.

Guaranteed to make you a better, more spiritual person

Available also in Bengali, Croatian, Gujarati, Hindi, Indonesian, Kannada, Malayalam, Marathi, Nepali, Polish, Russian, Slovene, Tamil, Telugu, and Urdu

Brahmacarya in Kṛṣṇa Consciousness

A "user's guide" to *brahmacārī* life. The first part consists of elaborate discussions and practical guidance regarding many aspects of *brahmacarya*. The second portion is a compilation of quotations on *brahmacarya* from Śrīla Prabhupāda's books, letters, and recordings.

Invaluable not only for *brahmacārīs* but for all devotees seriously interested in improving their spiritual life.

Available also in Bengali, Croatian, Gujarati, Hindi, Indonesian, Italian, Mandarin, Portuguese, Russian, Telugu, and Tamil

Glimpses of Traditional Indian Life

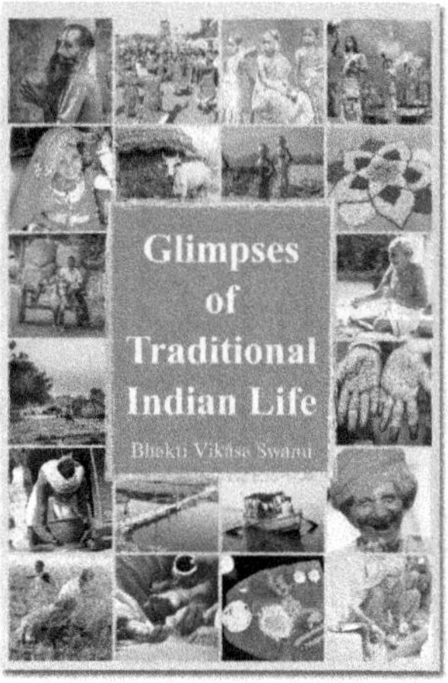

Journey to the real India. Discover the wisdom and devotion at the heart of Indian life. Meet people who were raised in a godly atmosphere and learn how it shaped their character and enriched their life. Explore the adverse effects of India's technological development, the downfall of her hereditary culture, and other causes of India's present degradation.

Available also in Croatian, Hindi, and Russian

Jaya Śrīla Prabhupāda!

There is no limit to Śrīla Prabhupāda's transcendental attributes, nor do we wish to ever stop describing them. His qualities, combined

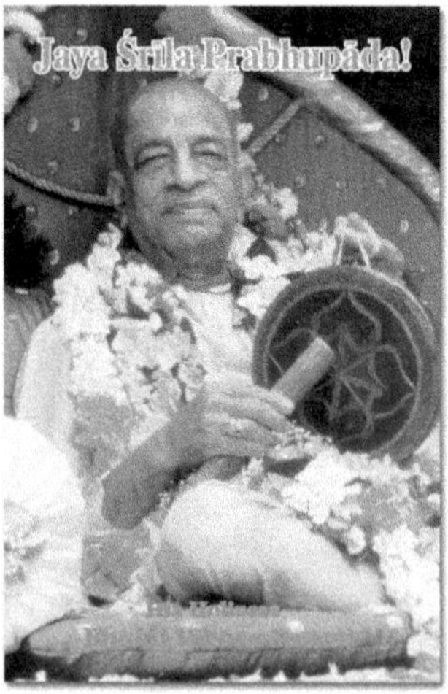

with his achievements, undoubtedly establish Śrīla Prabhupāda as an extraordinarily great transcendental personality.

Śrīla Prabhupāda is still with us, watching over the continuing expansion of the Kṛṣṇa consciousness movement. If we simply follow his instructions carefully, we can expect many amazing, unimaginable things to happen.

Available also in Gujarati, Russian, and Tamil

My Memories of Śrīla Prabhupāda

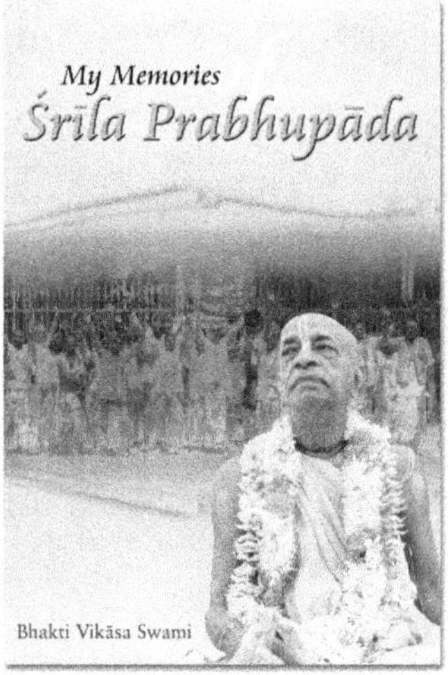

An ISKCON sannyasi recalls his few but precious memories of the most significant personality to have graced the earth in recent times.

Also includes:

- On Serving Śrīla Prabhupāda in Separation
- Vyasa-pūjā Offerings

Available also in Croatian, Gujarati, Hindi, and Russian

Rāmāyaṇa

Countless eons ago, when men and animals could converse together and powerful *brāhmaṇas* would effect miracles, the uncontrollable demon Rāvaṇa was terrorizing the universe. The *Rāmāyaṇa* records the adventures of Rāma, the Lord of righteousness, as He struggles to overcome the forces of Rāvaṇa. This absorbing narration has delighted and enlightened countless generations in India, and its timeless spiritual insights are compellingly relevant in today's confused world.

Available also in Croatian, Gujarati, Hindi, Kannada, Latvian, Marathi, Polish, Russian, Telugu, and Thai

Śrī Caitanya Mahāprabhu

Hundreds of thousands of people throughout the world now follow the spotless path of Kṛṣṇa consciousness as given by Lord Caitanya. Chanting the holy names of Kṛṣṇa and dancing in ecstasy, they desire only love of Kṛṣṇa and consider material enjoyment to be insignificant. This book gives an overview of the life and teachings of Śrī Caitanya Mahāprabhu, the most munificent avatar of God ever to grace this planet.

Available also in Gujarati, Hindi, Russian, Tamil, and Telugu

Śrī Vaṁśīdāsa Bābājī

Śrīla Vaṁśīdāsa Bābājī was a great Vaiṣṇava who although physically present in this world, had little communication with it. His hair and beard were uncut, matted, and dishevelled. He almost never bathed, and his eyes looked wild. He wore only a loin cloth, and nothing more.

This book introduces us to a personality of such extraordinary, inscrutable character that we simply offer him obeisance and beg for his mercy.

Available also in Croatian, Hindi, and Russian

Śrī Bhaktisiddhānta Vaibhava

Śrīla Bhaktisiddhānta Sarasvatī Ṭhākura altered the course of religious history by reviving and forcefully propagating pure Kṛṣṇa consciousness. His boldness in combating cheating religion earned him the appellation "lion guru"—yet his heart was soft with divine love for Kṛṣṇa.

Based in Bengal and traveling throughout India in the early twentieth century, Śrīla Bhaktisiddhānta Sarasvatī Ṭhākura laid the foundation for, and was the inspiration and guiding force behind, the later worldwide spreading of the Hare Kṛṣṇa movement.

The result of over twenty years of research, *Śrī Bhaktisiddhānta Vaibhava* presents a wealth of newly translated material. Replete with anecdotes told by disciples who lived with him, this devotional, philosophical, cultural, and historical study gives intimate insights into the activities, teachings, and character of an empowered emissary of the Supreme Lord.

Available also in Gujarati

On Pilgrimage in Holy India

Travel with an ISKCON sannyasi, including to some of India's less-known but most charming holy places.

Available also in Russian

The Story of Rasikānanda

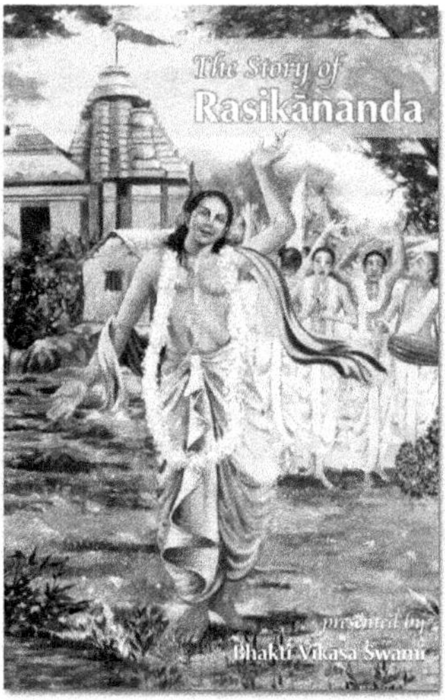

Śrī Rasikānanda Deva was a mighty Vaiṣṇava *ācārya* in the era after Lord Caitanya's disappearance. Along with his guru, Śrīla Śyāmānanda Paṇḍita, he inundated North Orissa and surrounding districts in waves of Kṛṣṇa-*prema* that are still flowing today. He subdued and converted atheists, blasphemers, and dacoits, and even tamed and initiated a rogue elephant! The exciting story of Śrī Rasikānanda Deva is told herein.

Available also in Gujarati, and Russian

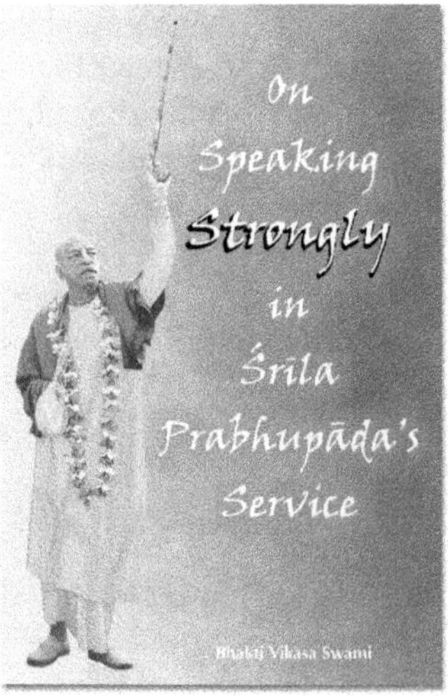

On Speaking Strongly in Śrīla Prabhupāda's Service

Why followers of Śrīla Prabhupāda should speak strongly, as he did. A comprehensive analysis of how to present Kṛṣṇa consciousness straightforwardly, intelligently, and effectively. Features many anecdotes and more than five hundred powerful quotes.

For more information, please visit: www.speakingstrongly.com

Available in English

Patropadeśa

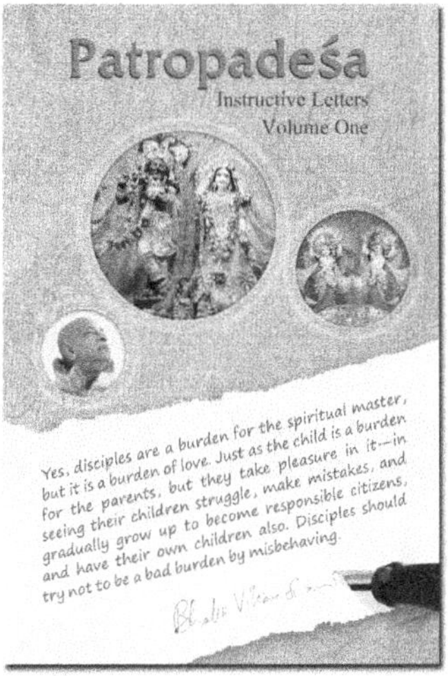

An anthology of selected correspondence with disciples and other devotees.

Packed with realistic advice on how to practice Kṛṣṇa consciousness in a complex world.

With many valuable philosophical insights and perspectives of guru-disciple interactions in the age of the internet.

Available in English

Mothers and Masters

Mothers and Masters presents traditionalist arguments for the direction of the Kṛṣṇa consciousness movement, proposing that we should take up Śrīla Prabhupāda's mandate to establish *varṇāśrama-dharma* rather than capitulate to the norms and ideologies of secular culture. Particularly discussed are gender roles, parental responsibilities, feminist follies, and some of Śrīla Prabhupāda's more controversial teachings, such as those concerning early marriage, divorce, and polygamy.

Available also in Hindi

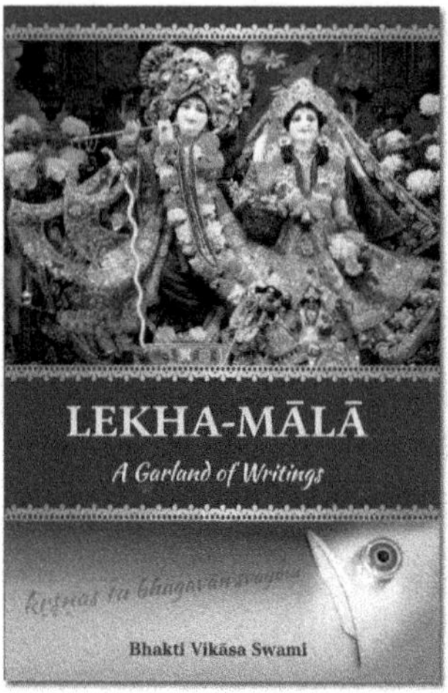

Lekha-māla

With over one and half million books in print in over twenty languages, Bhakti Vikāsa Swami is one of the most prolific and published writers on Kṛṣṇa consciousness in the world today. *Lekha-mālā* is a compilation of various of his writings that previously were unpublished or had not reached a wide audience. As with his other books, *Lekha-mālā* is informative, insightful, inspiring, and a pleasure to read.

Available in English

www.bvks.com

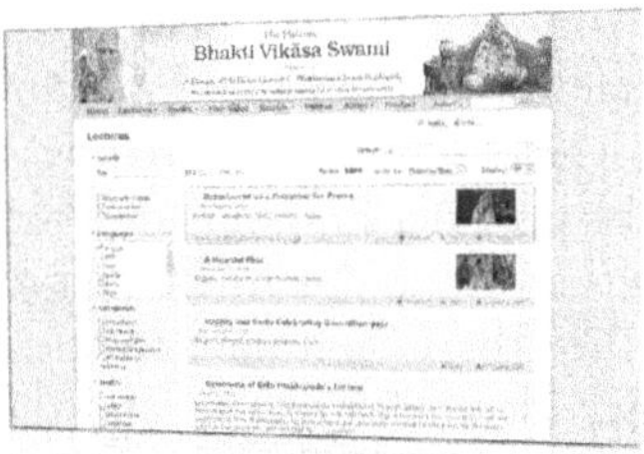

Listen online or download over 5,000 audio and 100 video lectures by Bhakti Vikāsa Swami in English, Bengali, and Hindi on *Bhagavad-gītā*, *Śrīmad-Bhāgavatam*, and various topics.

www.ingramcontent.com/pod-product-compliance
Lightning Source LLC
Chambersburg PA
CBHW070634030426
42337CB00020B/4014

* 9 7 8 8 1 9 0 8 2 9 2 3 6 *